BRITANNIA'S VOICES

SIXTY YEARS OF TRAINING AT DARTMOUTH

BRITANNIA'S VOICES

SIXTY YEARS OF TRAINING AT DARTMOUTH

JOSLIN FIENNES

This booklet is dedicated to those former naval cadets who were interviewed for this project, to the Navy they joined and to those who died in its service

Published by Britannia Museum Trust,
Britannia Royal Naval College, Dartmouth

First printed in the United Kingdom in 2017 by Gomer Press Ltd

Text copyright © 2017 Joslin Fiennes; illustrations © 2017 Britannia Museum and Archive and Britannia Royal Naval College unless otherwise attributed; and all quotations © 2017 respective contributors (listed in the Appendix)

Joslin Fiennes has asserted her right under the Copyright Designs and Patents Act 1988 to be identified as author of this work

Any opinions expressed by the author represent personal views and not those of any organisation or institution

All rights reserved

No part of this book may be reproduced, stored in a retrieval system, or transmitted in any form or by any means, electronic, mechanical, photocopying, recording, or otherwise, without the written permission of the publisher except for the purpose of research or private study, or criticism or review

ISBN: 978-1-5272-0871-1

Designed by Laura Parker, Paul Holberton Publishing

CONTENTS

SPONSORS 6

FOREWORD 7

INTRODUCTION 8

MEMORIES OF THE SECOND WORLD WAR 12

CHANGING TIMES 23

TRAINING 32

LEISURE 44

ENFORCING THE RULES 50

LEADERSHIP 58

THE REAL TEST OF TRAINING 67

APPENDIX AND PERSON INDEX 70

ACKNOWLEDGEMENTS AND RELATED INFORMATION 72

Grateful acknowledgement is given to The Heritage Lottery Fund and the Britannia Association for their support to the Oral History Project of the Britannia Museum Trust; and to The Foyle Foundation, the Britannia Royal Naval College Charities Committee and Nigel Way (The Royal Castle Hotel) for their support in the production of this booklet

FOREWORD

ADMIRAL OF THE FLEET, THE LORD BOYCE, KG, GCB, OBE, DL

This booklet is an important product of an exercise to collect the oral histories of a wide cross-section of cadets who were trained at Britannia Royal Naval College over 1930-1989. Not only does it give a fascinating insight into the social and political changes the country and the Navy saw over that time, but also how much at the College stayed the same, particularly in its emphasis on leadership that drew on long-standing history and traditions.

I well remember my own time as a cadet in the 1960s. The discipline, early morning activities and general hectic routine are still deeply ingrained, but perhaps I value the College most for being the start of a life-long sense of service and the deep friendships which this booklet so vividly evokes.

The Queen receiving a copy of the commemoration plate, 31st July, 1972, Prince Andrew watching

INTRODUCTION

This booklet is compiled from the memories of naval officer cadets who were at Britannia Royal Naval College in Dartmouth between 1930 and 1989. Sixty-five former cadets were interviewed over 2012–17, almost all over 2015–17 as part of the Oral History Project set up under the Britannia Museum Trust, which received major funding from the Heritage Lottery Fund and the Britannia Association. A list of interviewees is given in the appendix.

This is the first comprehensive collection of oral histories from ex-cadets, and the early memories of people now in their late 80s and 90s have particular historical interest. Recollections are all individual but six major themes emerge. The first, *Memories of the Second World War*, records what it was like to be training for the Navy when war was expected and then a reality. *Changing times* highlights how former cadets see their experiences with hindsight. *Training*, *Leisure* and *Enforcing the rules* show how they remember becoming naval officers. The final sections, *Leadership* and *The Real test of training* record the core purpose of the training and bring together memories of how it worked when tested in war.

Oral history is relived experience. And here it is history not by experts, but by people from all backgrounds, some of whom became important in the Navy, some who did not, and some who pursued quite different careers. It includes ex-cadets from abroad, the internationals, some 20 percent of the intake for most of the time.

College prospectuses for the 1930s–80s would tell us how it intended to train its cadets; these memories tell us what the training was like. They record how teambuilding and self-discipline was instilled, that role models worked and how an ethos of duty and service was developed. And they give a sense of the culture, the humour, the escapades and the friendships that made it all worthwhile. Even though these memories carry inevitable inaccuracies, distortions and gaps, they hold a truth that can be found nowhere else.

Looking back, those who knew, during the slow build-up of the 1930s, that they would go to war remember excitement, motivation and patriotism. Even in the worst days of the Battle of Britain and early defeats, even as cadets they knew were being killed and they themselves were being shot at on the river, they remember no doubts about winning. Surely some must have been terrified? We were young and naïve, they say, we were excited.

Beginning in the run-up to the Second World War and ending with the fall of the Berlin Wall, these interviews span an enormous change in the global roles of Britain and its Navy. Cadets from the first two decades were to serve in ships from Asia to the Atlantic and from the Arctic to the Antarctic when Britain had the second largest navy in the world. But its strength fell rapidly, from more than 860,000 naval personnel after the Second World War to 50,000 in the 1980s. By then, the Empire was long gone and we were well into the missile age.

From a school that recruited 13-year-olds for four years, the College became a technical naval institution in the mid-1950s and by the late 1980s was recruiting mainly graduates for a year. Fewer cadets were being trained for far fewer ships with far more sophisticated engineering and weaponry. By 1988 the average age of cadets was 23 and 73 percent had degrees. Interviewees saw recruitment becoming more meritocratic and as the age of entry rose and attitudes generally changed, corporal punishment ceased. Women arrived, but even in the 1980s they were trained for subordinate positions and – as one former WRNS said, "it seems so weird now" – encouraged to be feminine.

While the details vary, the memories that dominate recur across all the decades. These involve remorseless pressure to keep to timetables and run everywhere. All remember the drilling on the parade ground, learning seamanship and playing sports. And discipline, the self-discipline that comes from keeping to the rules when you'd rather not – wear

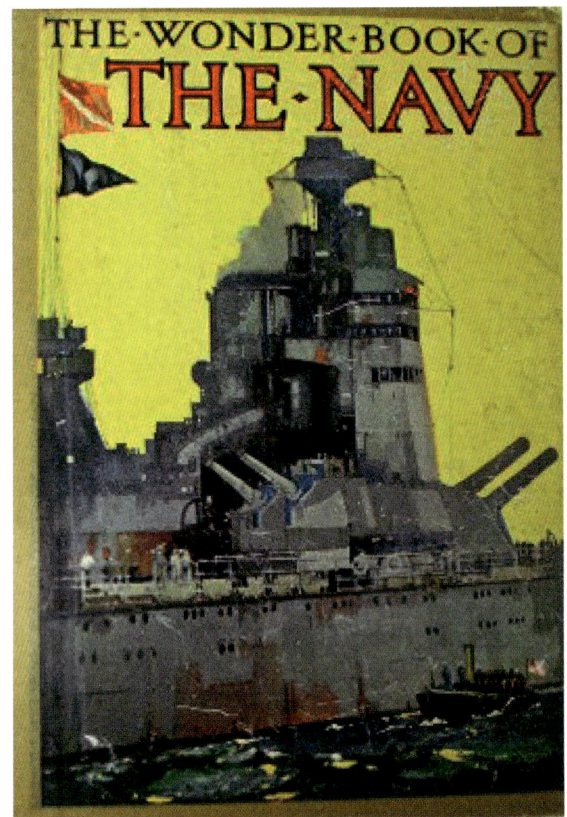

Many ex-cadets remember being attracted to the Navy by books

the right rig at the right time, and keep those clothes tidy – and the discipline that happens when you don't.

Listening to the memories of these cadets you hear the voices of people who were active, rugby players, who enjoyed the water, the sort who remembered just getting on with things, whether it was early morning exercises or parades in the cold and the rain. Even the 13-year-olds were reluctant to admit to feelings, tending to remember homesickness in others, although there were striking exceptions.

There were always rebels. Corporal punishment in the early years became a badge of honour, undermining its effect. Some confronted the system or negotiated deals. Several found that the system tolerated some high spirits that broke the rules, as long as they didn't go to extremes. You could fly your Tiger Moth low over the College – once.

Former cadets remember with affection inspirational or just eccentric teachers and petty officers. Early cadets who spent longer at the College recall Sunday cream teas, watching Mark Sugden play poetic rugby, the radio club and ballroom dancing with other cadets. Some can still quote their French teacher, in French. Later cadets had escapades with cars, motorbikes and girls. Almost everyone looks back with pleasure on the river, HRH The Duke of Edinburgh recalling how much he enjoyed skippering boats on the Dart and out at sea. And all delight in talking of awful times on Dartmoor and Oily Q's, their name for the "officer-like qualities" they were expected to display.

But, even now, some ex-cadets are still irritated by parts of their training. Teaching seamanship with funny little models rather than on board ship, for example. Or "the bullshit end of training" like polishing boots and being too rigid about trivia. Other complaints were never seeing ratings when you were being trained to lead them and giving WRNS officer cadets make-up classes in the 1980s, when Margaret Thatcher was Prime Minister.

Despite the changes in the Navy, these memories of how the College produced leaders tell us that essential aspects have endured. Civilians are becoming naval officers as they always have, through practice, learning from mistakes and through role models, being trained in self-discipline, teamwork and good judgement. As HRH Prince Andrew sees it, "Dartmouth has been able to manoeuvre itself to deliver that change from being a civilian to a serviceman, whatever the needs, whether it's a 13-year-old, or, as my case as a 19-year-old, to a 23-year-old." The College has remained true to its purpose.

You would recognise these former cadets. Neatly dressed, with accents modified for clarity (elocution was still taught at the College in the 1980s), most are excessively punctual by civilian standards, and still fold their clothes neatly. They are contributors to society – being magistrates, running local charities and standing for local office. Almost all have deep friendships born of the intense experiences at Dartmouth.

JOSLIN FIENNES

Sandbags against D-block during the Munich crisis

MEMORIES OF THE SECOND WORLD WAR

In 1933 Hitler came to power in Germany. The Germans occupied the Rhineland in 1936 and two years later annexed Austria. Cadets joining the Naval College in the 1930s and 1940s have strong memories of war and its impending threat. They mostly came as 13-year-olds and were in their 80s and 90s when they were interviewed. What they say shows how clearly they remember that time, recalling details such as dates and names as well as how they felt and thought about their training and their future.

Anthony McCrum, who joined in 1932 for four years, remembers that Munich in 1938 changed him from being a pacifist:

> I knew some time in the next year or so we would be at war. ... It didn't frighten me. I just thought it was essential. By that time having been almost a pacifist I just thought that Hitler was evil. ... Jewish children were coming to this country. We were told about the horrors of killing small children with Downs Syndrome. We knew a lot about the beating up of the Jews, the smashing of their shops. It was quite enough to know that the Nazi system was thoroughly evil.

No cadets arriving after 1938 could be in any doubt that war was coming. James Jungius, 1930s, describes "building barriers of sandbags around the College in case it was bombed during the Munich crisis." And he recalls the College being invaded by stranded soldiers on a pre-war exercise:

> In about 1938/1939 ... the army conducted a landing exercise on Slapton Sands [along the coast from Dartmouth]. A brigade of soldiers ... all got ashore and then a terrible gale blew up and they couldn't re-embark. Two or three thousand soldiers were left stranded ... with the rain pouring down and no way of getting back to their ships. ... And so they came to the College [which] put them up for the night. ... We had soldiers sleeping all down the corridors ... and we gave them a hot meal and breakfast ... They were commanded by Montgomery who I think was then a Brigadier, but could have been a Major General. And as a thank you to the College ... he presented a very nice little statue of a soldier ... which I imagine is still there. ... [Sadly, it's not.]

"There was never any doubt about winning"

There was an urge to get moving. "By the time September 1939 came along," recalls McCrum, "I think many of us had got to the point where we said let's get on with it. ... Let's get it over."

For McCrum, going to war was a matter of conscience. For Rolfe Monteith, a Special Entry from Canada who was 17 when he came in 1941, it was an adventure (Special Entry was an early entry system for older cadets that ended in the mid-1950s):

> I was a young, naïve person from the middle of Canada. I had no sophistication. I didn't really understand the real world ... I was on a frolic almost. ... For the Canadians to be in a wartime area, black-out, troops everywhere, and activity related to the war, was fabulous. It was a whole fresh world that we entered. ... I was given brown overalls and a gas mask which ... I don't think we were even instructed in. But we had one put on our chest with a steel helmet. And I was selected to have a rifle ... And of course we all grew up. ... I was just 17 ... naïve and innocent ... It would be a super [experience] for young people today. ... We left that College absolutely part of a wartime machine.

Many cadets felt excitement combined with an absolute faith in victory, despite Germany's steady advances in Europe after Munich, the occupation of Czechoslovakia and the Russo-German Pact. "Even in the worst days," says McCrum, "there was never any doubt about winning, funnily enough."

And James Jungius remembers optimism that persisted even after the disastrous events of 1940, the invasions of northern Europe and then France, the fall of Dunkirk and the Battle of Britain: "I was never in any doubt that we were going to win. Totally illogical because we weren't doing at all well. ... Even when quite a lot of ships were sunk, I still thought we were going to win. ... Quite a few of us felt like that I think."

Not all were initially so confident. Halfway through his time at Dartmouth, Adrian Holloway, who joined in 1936, began to realise that "the Navy was not my métier", but he felt he couldn't leave. "War was approaching, and it was quite obvious that soon we would go to sea. ... In those days, if you wanted to leave Dartmouth, your parents had to pay a forfeit, quite a substantial one I think, unless you got kicked out ... and so one stayed."

But he was galvanised as war became imminent: "you hoped, although [you were] a very small cog in the wheel, that you might be some use in fighting Hitler. And so the nearer we got to 1939, we felt there that there was some purpose in life."

So excitement, yes, but also apprehension. John Forbes, who joined in 1939, remembers being "keen that the war was still going on [yet also] ... apprehensive. Was I going to be able to do what I was supposed to do? And I think it was the same with all of us. We knew we were missing out on the two terms in the training cruiser, were we going to be able to cope when we went to sea?"

Remembering major events

Cadets remembered where they were and what they were doing when war was declared. James Jungius recalls: "I was actually on leave … down in Cornwall. I remember with my parents listening to the announcement that we were now at war. And I walked along the cliffs and had a swim, thinking I wonder where this is going to take me. But possibly a bit of excitement – gosh here we go."

William O'Brien, 1930s, was at sea:

> I was navigator of a destroyer on patrol off Perim at the bottom of the Red Sea … in case the Italians came in. I was on watch. It was [about] three o'clock in the afternoon [there]. … And this chap shouted up from the wireless office 'Message number so and so' which one knew immediately meant war was declared. I leant over the bridge to the captain who was on the sponson on the flag deck below me reading a book in a deckchair. And I said 'Captain, Sir' and he said 'Yes?' I said 'War's declared.' He took his eyeglass out of his eye and said 'Thank you very much', put it back in and went back to reading his book.

Then came the invasion of France. "Really, quite honestly, we longed to get to sea," says Adrian Holloway. "And then, of course, there came the invasion of France, and that really galvanised the whole place."

The invasion was followed by the destruction of the French Navy, an event remembered with great emotion by Rolfe Monteith, who "had extremely close links with the French":

> They served with us. … I was next to Cyril Herbout, of the Free French Navy, in a hammock at the Naval College. Absolutely brilliant chap. The war ended, I was walking down Piccadilly and there's Cyril Herbout. Suddenly, big hugs. Cyril, how are you? 'Well,' he said, 'I want to tell you a little story.' … [To] cut down on a lot of the detail, he said 'the war finished May 1945.' He made his way back to his village. He'd been away five years. Walked up the steps of his home. Banged on the door. The door opened and it was his father. His father said to him 'traitor!' and slammed the door. … I feel sorry for France. They had a strange war, I may be getting this off my chest [but] … the British had been forced to shell the French fleet [in Oran] just after Europe had fallen. Churchill said 'bombard the fleet. That's an order!' And … that's what convinced Roosevelt the British were serious about the war. So that was a huge turning point. Two thousand Frenchmen were killed. A lot of French serving officers held the view, maybe rightly, maybe wrongly, that that was a horrendous thing for an ally to do.

Retreads, blackouts and getting on with it

The threat of war increased cadet numbers, as Anthony McCrum remembers: "The rearmament programme [had] started in full flood by 1936. Lots more ships, huge increase in the 18-year-old entry from public schools because you couldn't ... increase the Dartmouth entry very quickly because they took nearly four years." At the same time, training time was shortened. "We didn't go the two terms that we used to before going to sea in the training cruiser. ... We went straight to sea from our 11th term at Dartmouth," says John Forbes.

Teachers left too and were replaced with retirees. Adrian Holloway, who left in 1940, was in his ninth term when war was declared: "which meant I had two more to go in September 1939. ... All the peacetime officers had disappeared and in their place were what we called 'retreads', older officers who had been retired and came back to act as house officers."

And Monteith says with affection:

> At Dartmouth, the Commanding Officer was [only] a Lieutenant Commander ... drawn back in from retirement and ... the officers and particularly the chief petty officers, had all left the Navy years before. ... I have the highest respect for those people detailed off to train us, because they'd been brought back from probably lovely retirement.

Wartime adjustments were made, as John Forbes describes:

> All the windows were blacked out. Food and milk were rationed ... As the years went on, there were more and more air raid alarms and we used to have to go down to the passages below the College ... which were hot and sticky and a lot of us had used for smoking before. They were awful ... we had our chests in the dormitories but we slept in the boot rooms which were semi-underground. ... They were airless and we made them even more airless by putting sandbags all around them. The senior people provided fire watching during air raid alarms.

"There were machine guns on the roof, not that I think they did much good, and we began to dig trenches," recalls Holloway. While Monteith remembers that "if the Germans arrived we were instructed to do whatever occurred to us as being sensible. People on either side of me had a wooden ... pole. That was their weapon. My weapon was a 303 rifle with no ammunition."

How much were these 13- to 17-year-old cadets taught about the war? "Our house officer was Lieutenant Commander 'Pluffy' Plowden whose job in peacetime had been with the BBC," says Holloway. "He used to bring his radio into the gunroom and we would listen to Churchill's speeches, cheer him to the echo."

But the College was still a school, with a very pressured syllabus described below, and Holloway remembers, basically, just having to get on with things:

> We looked at the newspapers every day. The Battle of Britain had not yet begun. That happened in my leave when I had left Dartmouth. And you really just took things as they came. ... You lived a rather

enclosed existence and, to be honest, our days were so full. After all, we were patrolling the streets of Dartmouth and manning the gun, but we still had to take all our exams. And by that time, we were being taught signals and gunnery and torpedoes and this that and the other, and no allowance was made for all that, you just got on with it. So we were so darned occupied that I don't think we had any thoughts about [the war].

Forbes has similar memories of unchanged daily routines: "Everything went on the same. The instruction was the same. I felt that perhaps we could be taught a bit more about the war … . But we weren't. We just ticked along basically, academically just like any other school and on the naval side we ticked along the same way as we had before war was declared."

Small eddies of bigger tides

Cadets remember many small events at Dartmouth that tied them into the increasing global turmoil. The smell of unwashed bodies on the quarterdeck and Belgian, French and Dutch trawlers slipping into Dartmouth harbour at night brought home to Holloway that the Germans were winning in northern Europe:

> The first intimation that war had really struck us was when … I walked into the quarterdeck one morning and there was an awful fetid smell, which later I was to recognise [as that of] unwashed men's bodies. The quarterdeck was littered with men in dirty, mud-spattered uniforms, all of them absolutely asleep. … I suddenly realised that these were your British expeditionary force who'd been completely defeated by Hitler. And that brought it home to me. The next thing that happened was that the harbour, one night, became full of trawlers, Belgian, French and Dutch [fishermen], who'd brought their families with them.

And just as the rest of England began to address the possibility of invasion, Holloway remembers the panic, and being sent out to patrol the streets of Dartmouth and man the castle while a torpedo tube was built in Kingswear:

> It was thought that fifth columnists might be among [the fishermen]. Of course … it was absolute rubbish. [But] we were ordered to patrol the darkened streets of Dartmouth, with fixed bayonets and rifles on our shoulders. Once … some cadet was so frightened that instead of 'Halt, who goes there?' he shouted out 'Halt, there he goes!' … We were ordered to man a gun at Dartmouth castle. The gun, of course, had been produced by the Japanese, but we didn't know it at the time. We had all these shells, which were merely under a canvas covering. And we slept in tents there. … It was beautiful weather. We had … Cornish pasties brought out from the College and lived a really rather idyllic life. …One Stuka could've wiped us out completely. And then they built a torpedo tube in Kingswear. The whole thing was ridiculous

The statue of King George V had only minor damage after the bombing of the quarterdeck

because no enemy, I think, would ever have landed in Dartmouth. …The entrance was so narrow, they'd have gone to Slapton, which was where the D-Day exercises took place.

But Dartmouth did see action. The Naval College was a landmark, standing high on a ridge above the town, and it was a target for the Germans. John Treacher, who arrived in 1939, recalls:

I was actually on the river when we were shot at. And the aircraft came over, six of them. … Chief Petty Officer Savage, we always said that he lived up to his name … was in charge. He got us to lie on the bottom of the boat under the seats because they did a second strafing. It was all over in 15 minutes. … The Admiralty said: 'We stopped them going to sea because we didn't want to lose our men … and now we're going to lose them if we leave them down here.'

"Two of them took the College"

John Davies was on the river when the College was bombed on 18th September 1942:

During the last week of summer leave … I was … on the Dart between Dittisham and Dartmouth when these planes came in over Galmpton. … They … flew low down the river in pairs, and two of them took the College. By the time anyone could do anything, they were already on their way home.

Was he scared? His reply was laconic: "Well, I'd seen so much of it already. When I was up near Liverpool we had a lot of bombing. There was a war on. There were ships, motor torpedo boats and raiding craft in and out of the river all the time. There was a lot of naval activity on the Dart." Did it make him angry? "No." So what did he do? "I just sailed back up the river … ."

During the same raid, 23 people were killed at the nearby shipyard and one Wren was killed at the College. John Forbes recalls how the cadets had had a very lucky escape:

Commemorative plaque to Ellen Whittall, a Wren, the only person killed at the College during the bombing raid, installed in 2005. Photo by Jane Harrold

Just before my last term in the summer we had a week's extra leave, which only happened every six years for some reason. And it was just … in that week the College was bombed. If we had gone back on the normal date at least 250 cadets would have been killed by … the bombs dropped on the quarter deck. [After the bombing] the junior half of the College disappeared off to an orphanage in Bristol, leaving the top five or six terms behind. I was in … my 11th term. … Most of the classrooms around the quarterdeck couldn't be used so we were taught in all kinds of places like squash courts and the masters' hostel. Instead of having parades on the quarterdeck when it rained, we had them in the main passage. … I got presented, before going off to sea, with I think it was the last king's dirk.

"Certainly a third were killed"

Of the cadets from Dartmouth who went to war in those early years, about a third lost their lives. "We suffered terribly in the war, because we were then sub-lieutenants," says Duncan Knight, who left in 1937. "We were absolute cannon fodder. The Fleet Air Arm and submarines claimed a lot of my term. I think we lost … about 30 per cent."

And James Jungius who passed out in 1940 remembers the same high losses:

> I haven't got the exact figures but I think of my term at least a third or possibly more … were killed. … One of my term was on *HMS Hood* when it was sunk [with] only three survivors out of a crew of 800. … We went to sea at the end of 1940 and beginning of 1941 when there were quite a lot of losses in the Mediterranean. … I lost my best friend, nice chap. He was an only child of a widowed mother, very much the apple of her eye, which was a terrible thing, but there we are.

The Eaton Hall years

In February 1943, after the bombing of the Naval College in Dartmouth, it re-opened at the Duke of Westminster's home, Eaton Hall in Cheshire, where it was to remain until September 1946 when it returned to Dartmouth.

Although everyone had family who was affected and faced the war directly when they went home, Eaton Hall was secluded and safer than Dartmouth. "Thank goodness, we weren't being bombed, just

Eaton Hall, Blake Line Book sketch by cadet in 1946

six miles south of Chester," says Patrick Harland, who arrived in 1943. "And then of course when the V1s and V2s came, it really only affected the south of England, and London."

What was it like? "Tough! ... Pretty horrendous really, but we survived." Harland went on:

> For your first two terms you lived in the ... Duke of Westminster's main house where ... there were dormitories ... But later ... you had to go to hutted camps. ... In fact I think all the classrooms were in huts, which had great big coke boilers to keep them warm. ... There were ... a lot of grounds where we could play games and we had the River Dee where we could do a bit of sailing. Not as good as on the Dart of course. ... The whole College ate in a ... shed.

But there was a bright side. Instead of the sandbags and patrolling of Dartmouth, William Melly, who came in 1943, even remembers: "When you were in the 11th term you were allowed into Chester at weekends. And there was a tea dance establishment at Chester called Quaintways. We used to arrange to happen to meet a Wren [to dance with] at Quaintways. ... I think they knew it went on."

"We hoped we would get to sea"

War had already started for the cadets joining the Navy in the 1940s. Like those who had joined earlier, these were the cadets who had chosen to serve in the Navy knowing they would probably have to go to war and risk paying the ultimate price. In fact those joining after mid-1942 did not, but they did not know this for some three years. Harland recalls:

> We just had no idea whether we would get into the war or not. Certainly I think we ... joined in the first place because we were keen to go and fight for our country. It was an amazing patriotism in those days. Obviously people like me who had elder brothers who were involved hoped we would get to sea before the end of the war. In fact we didn't. ... We had our last two terms at Dartmouth and then went to the training cruiser but it was all over by then.

The war was all around these cadets and had a profound effect on their lives. "I think everybody had some connection with the sadness of the war," says Rodney Agar, 1940s:

Sailing on the River Dee at Eaton Hall

Every family suffered in one way or another, friends of ours had two sons who were killed on the same day. ... even at my prep school boys' fathers were being killed, and at Dartmouth I remember somebody in the term below me, his father was killed. But you know, it was something that you accepted ... you had to live with it, and that was it.

These later cadets would have known about the heavy losses being suffered by their predecessors at the College. Many have memories of losing friends, but Patrick Harland's story of Bill Linton, whose father was captain of a submarine, is exceptionally poignant:

When we joined our first term, [Bill] heard that his father had been killed. ... He had won the VC and DSO and DSC and poor old Bill, aged 13, had to go up and collect them from Buckingham Palace. Obviously his mother was there as well. ... Bill ... decided to specialise in submarines and he ... went to sea ... in a submarine called *Affray* that sank ... between the Isle of Wight and the Channel Islands. All on board perished, [including] ... six in my term and three more from the term above. ... It took weeks to find [*Affray*]. ... It had just gone out on a training exercise, [to give] these sub-lieutenants experience of going to sea in a submarine to see what it was like. It was really traumatic.

At this stage, many of the staff had fought in the war and ex-cadets, looking back, remember their names and decorations and how much they were admired. Some, Harland recalls, talked about the war:

Each house ... had a house officer who was a serving Lieutenant Commander in the Navy, and he certainly used to speak to us, I think about once a week ... and would certainly have kept us up to speed on what was going on in the war. ... My house officer in Hawke for my last few terms was highly decorated, and had a DSO and an OBE and a DSC. ... One really stood a bit in awe of a guy like that because he had achieved so much and yet he was only about 30.

Reading between the lines, staff at the College were wary of too much war-talk. William Melly remembers the teachers who had fought but didn't talk about it. He remembers a house officer " Peter Dickins, DSO and bar and DSC and two bars, who'd been a big motor torpedo boatman with Peter Scott and people like that." But, he goes on, "they talked about it very little. Maybe they'd been told not to, otherwise we'd get frightened." Anyway, he comments, cadets had so much academic work. "We were too busy learning about the Battle of Trafalgar." Melly seems to have learnt about the progress of the war from newspapers lying about.

Were cadets aware of the full implications of joining a fighting force? Jolyon Waterfield, arriving in 1947, wasn't sure they were ever really explained:

How many of us have woken up and realised that a fighting force is exactly that, and that we had to be prepared to kill other people and put our lives on the line as well? And I just wonder [whether] ... that was ever pointed out to me. ... I'm not even sure when I went back on the staff at Dartmouth [in 1964], by which time trainees were arriving at the ... minimum age of 18, whether it was put to them.

After the first two dreadful years of defeat in Europe and Asia and the Battle of Britain, the tide of the war began to change. Despite knowing of the Navy's continuing losses, cadets at the College from 1943 were aware of the naval victories in the Pacific and victories in El Alamein and Stalingrad. In their memories you sense a new hope and, above all, patriotism and excitement, and wonder that the war was won.

"I think," recalls Patrick Harland, "because you were in a naval environment the whole time, it was ... marvellous. You had great impetus during the war because you thought you were going to go out and fight anyway. People were amazingly patriotic back in those days, I can't describe to you how. I mean it was incredible that we won that war."

And the tide changed
Cadets passing out after the war ended were deeply aware of the courage and dedication of those who had fought. Murray Johnstone, who passed out in 1946, remembers the peace celebrations when the College had moved back to Dartmouth and paid a tribute to those who had fought:

We had a parade that was attended by the commander-in-chief, Plymouth. He and all the staff of course had fought in the world war, and we hadn't. We were aware of it needless to say, and all the terrible things which occurred. ... They [deserved anything] they wanted if they'd fought in the war and we hadn't. ... I went to a ... battleship ... full of troops ... who had fought ... and you couldn't help but be impressed by the dedication of people who'd given everything they had ... saving themselves and everybody else. And that couldn't help but impress you. You realised that you joined something which was worthwhile.

CHANGING TIMES

"We were in a totally different world to today's"
Many cadets commented on how the world they knew at Dartmouth has changed. The role of the Navy has been revolutionised since the 1930s. James Jungius:

> When I joined Dartmouth in May 1937 the Royal Navy was still the largest Navy in the world. Britain still ruled about half the world, and there wasn't an ocean ... where British warships were not stationed. We had gunboats up the Yangtze. Once or twice a week in the papers there would be a little item showing where HM ships were. *HMS York* arrived in Hong Kong, *HMS Newcastle* something else and something else departed from Buenos Aires and so on.

As the Navy changed, so did the training. David Carpenter, comparing 1965 with 1974:

> In 1965 I joined the Dartmouth Training Squadron that was a reflection of the Navy of both my father and Nelson. Rum was still served, though not to cadets, we slept in hammocks, we went away in a sea boat and it was in all respects crews with the three ships in competition either sailing, in harbour or keeping station on each other. By the time I returned in 1974, we had well and truly entered the missile age. The College was structured differently and the Dartmouth Training Squadron was one ship, an assault carrier, a capital ship, with very many fewer tasks for the cadets to perform in terms of seamanship. We didn't sleep in hammocks, rum had gone and it was altogether a different atmosphere.

Instead of recruiting 13-year-olds, the College brought in cadets first at 16, then 18, and then older. Jock Morrison, 1950s, regretted the change in ethos as officer cadets no longer joined the Navy for life:

> The people ... trained entirely to meet the Navy's requirements [were] about service, commitment, taking the pay and ... it's forever. Whereas I get the impression that today's young officers join most often with a degree ... and as they join they are busy looking at the next job opportunity outside the Navy. You don't run a war that way.

Training at Dartmouth when it was a traditional school. Compare with the photograph opposite

But for Carpenter, a specialist Navy that is no longer a lifetime career works: "By the time I left we were in the 21st-century Navy, with flexible working that one would never have thought possible when I first joined. But it works ... for the officer, it works for the Navy. It is very useful for specialist officers and ratings who want to remain in one niche, engineering perhaps, without being posted away."

As the Navy downsized, entries became smaller, and Terry Jane, comparing the late 1960s with the early 1980s, remembered how it changed the whole feel of the place: "When I was there ... everywhere you went ... there were dozens if not tens of dozens of ... people rushing in all directions. When I went back on the staff, I well remember ... walking down that very long corridor at the very front and not seeing anybody."

And he found that although cadets were older:

> Interestingly enough they were less confident ... they'd actually only been in the service a very short time, some of them months effectively, whereas in my time sub-lieutenants had been in the Navy three years. ... They were much more likely to ... start running round asking 'how do I do it?' We would never have done that ... We'd just do it and if it didn't work find another way.

The demise of class
The Attlee reforms of 1948 aimed to abolish fees and broaden the intake – to change its class. Rupert Craven, on the College in the 1930s: "Dartmouth was a self-perpetuating, middle class organisation. Now, I'm by no means a socialist. In fact, I'm probably a threatened species, I'm a Tory in Scotland. But ... it's ridiculous to recruit officers only from one particular area. Most particularly is it a mistake."

Tom Potts, an early scholarship cadet in the 1940s, remembers being different, but not for long: "I'd always lived at home and ... most of the other cadets joining at that time had been to boarding schools. But I fitted in very well almost immediately you know. If you can't beat them, join them ... I was a very quiet boy. I just watched what everyone else did and copied them really. And then of course we had a very busy routine and you didn't have much time to think."

Jonathan Tod, there in the 1950s, only saw change in the intake 20 years later:

A modern language class in the 1980s

year olds who were just getting on with ... learning how to be naval officers. So I don't think the class distinction, if indeed it existed then, made ... any difference at all."

Mark Barton, 1980s, believes the Attlee changes have finally borne fruit and that class has been superseded by merit as a basis for promotion:

> We no longer attract the class [we did and] ... freedom of movement between classes is much easier now. ... I have got junior sailors in my department who went to boarding school and are the social equal of my junior officers. The difference now is your academics and your leadership qualities, not your social class. And that is a real change over my career.

Elocution: class and clarity

Accents were a signal of class, and the Navy gave elocution lessons. John Madgwick, from Canada, expected to have trouble in the 1960s. He didn't, but recorded: "Young people from Glasgow and the north east were required to do elocution lessons. ... Their accents changed quite remarkably over the 12-month period." And in the 1970s Christopher Ayres remembers: "One guy had quite a strong Liverpool accent [and] got invited to go to elocution lessons ... I'm sure that wouldn't happen today. The ideal accent was very neutral ... in those days."

People could become self-conscious about just those accents that the Navy accepted. Richard Hill, 1940s, found he was resented in a later career for the

Dartmouth [in the 1950s] was just a continuation of the British public school system. ... I have spent some time trying to think of the people in my term who had been to other than public schools. And quite frankly, I can only think of one. ... I'm sure there were more ... but the percentage was very, very small. When I was back as an instructor it had changed round completely. To find a public school boy there was really rather hard in the 1970s ...

Several people found that mixing up the classes at Dartmouth helped to defuse the whole issue. Andrew Craig, Australian, 1960s: "When all the dust settled we all turned out to be perfectly similar 19-20 way he spoke: "Some people say [I have] a very nice voice, [but] more … say it's a toffee-nosed voice and I talk down to people … I got on in the Navy far more quickly and easily than I did in Shell, entirely due to this wretched educated voice I've got."

By the 1980s, Henry Duffy relished the fact that anyone who didn't speak clearly had to do what was then called effective communication training:

> There was a chap, a friend of mine now, who came to ECT. I had this broad Liverpudlian accent, and he had the most clipped southern counties accent, sounded like the Queen Mum's lost cousin. … And he was there not because he had a regional accent, it was because no-one could understand him because he was posh … I loved the idea that he had to be there as well.

But a sort of professional snobbery persisted. The Attlee Government had aimed to recruit 25 percent of officers from the lower deck, but, as Cliff Williams, an Upper Yardman who had been a senior rating, records, he still faced prejudice in the 1970s. He was expected to relinquish any "lower-deck attitude", which involved showing "you had left the rating's way of life … and started afresh … and even that you had left [your old friends] on the lower deck behind." He remembered that a friend who had also been an Upper Yardman and was at the College "invited me to come … to have a look around. … He was accused of having a lower-deck attitude. That went against him. He should have left me and all his other friends behind because … he had moved on. … It was quite a step from being a rating to being an officer."

Nichola Winstanley recognised the hint of prejudice in the 1980s:

> The only prejudice, [which] … didn't manifest itself particularly, was the fact that you hadn't gone through public school education. And that your parents weren't professional people. So my father … was an engineer, and he worked at a toothbrush factory. And my mother had been a dinner lady. And I used to take a certain satisfaction and pride in saying 'that's what they are, but they've encouraged me, they have provided me with the same opportunities as anybody else.'

"I went at the age of six"

As the age of entry rose, there were fewer memories of homesickness. Some of the early cadets recalled it only in others. William O'Brien, there in the 1930s, even said: "I had three siblings. They were all away at school and I badgered my mother to get me to school, because I was bored without them. So I went at the age of six."

But some did remember. Derek Willan, 1930: "I think it probably was a lonely place. But, you are kept occupied for so much of the time it probably didn't sink in as much as it otherwise might have done."

And Anthony Fletcher talks about a kind tutor in the 1930s but his description of his time is permeated with loneliness:

I was on my own very much. My father was away in China, and my mother was not well mentally. I wrote … formal letters, very careful not to say Mummy or Daddy … I had one sister about three and a half years younger than me who now lives in Australia and whom I love very much but at the time I called her 'It'.

Generally speaking, I messed about and I didn't [do] as much work as I should have done. I was always at the back and I never spoke at all if I could help it because I had a slight stammer. … I was afraid of standing up in front of people and … very anxious when I had to give commands …

When I was about 13 and I had been there about three weeks I knew one chap really well. I came down with mumps and I was put into a whole wing of the hospital by myself. … On one occasion I was visited by the padre and [asked about] … a lot of activity opposite … He said 'Oh yes, Gordon died. Didn't you know?' And of course, Gordon was the only boy I knew really … I was all by myself and as I had a lot of song books I was able to sing my way through. … I was told that I ought to read poetry. It was my first introduction to death.

But Colin Traill, one of the last 13-year-olds in the 1950s, remembers frequent letter-writing to his mother and a watchful padre: "I wrote reassuring letters and she wrote cheerful letters back and so did my father. … The padre wrote to my parents after about 4-6 weeks, reassuring them that I wasn't sobbing in my bed every night. So one was looked after."

Former cadets at the College in the 1970s and 1980s did talk about homesickness, but they were older, more independent and many had already made the break from home. Mark Barton, 1980s:

I don't remember people taking particular interest … if you were homesick . … Your peers would try to talk you round, but it was a different era in many ways. … You were much more isolated, and you just had to park that outside life and live the life that was there. … I didn't go home even for my half term break from Dartmouth. … I was quite determined when I joined that I was breaking [from home].

The passing of the beating and the yelling

Ideas about discipline evolved particularly radically. In the 1930s, James Jungius points out: "Corporal punishment was not unique to the Navy by a long way. Practically all public schools and prep schools indulged in corporal punishment. Nobody thought it was terrible. Parents smacked their children. It was a different world."

And cadets remember they didn't question their situation as they might today. Paul Rampling, 1980s: "In my day most of us were non-graduates [and just thought] … this is what it is. You don't argue with it, you just get on with it. … Nowadays people … question a lot more."

As the age and education of the intake rose, corporal punishment became unworkable. And the house captains remember refusing to administer it anyway. Joe Young, in the 1950s, who joined at 18 from a state school: "House captains … were allowed to administer beatings if they thought they were deserved. We 18-year-olds thought it was unbelievably ridiculous and out of date to a man. Really, really bad." Did he beat anyone? "No, I wouldn't, honestly. … You can make people do things without having to do that. … Don't think it did a lot of good. It brought out the worst in people, I suspect."

John Lippiett remembers verbal abuse in the 1960s that wouldn't be allowed today. He reports that when his youngest son was training for the Guards: "if the Sergeant bellowed at someone … they would go and complain to the … platoon commander, my son … and he'd have to investigate it." Lippiett records that for him:

> Verbal abuse was a matter of course … on the parade ground or in the gym. It was very funny, actually, but it would not be permitted [today]. … We learned a lot of language … from both our gunnery instructors, who really were the heart and soul of our life in certainly the first term, and the acting sub-lieutenants … and then the divisional officers.

Neil Blair, in the 1950s, pointed out: "If there were a group of clever graduates in the gunroom doing basic naval training you couldn't quite shout at them in the same way as you had 20 years before. In their minds they'd say … we're not going to respond to this kind of mindless disciplinary behaviour that you think you ought to instil."

But those who suffered from harsh discipline often regretted its passing. Lippiett again: "It was brutal … but harmless, and character forming, as opposed to character destroying." He goes on: "and actually that's very good training. I think Dartmouth now probably is too soft." And Adrian Holloway: "I was a magistrate for 30 years and I think it would have been a damn good thing if a lot of the young chaps who came up before me were beaten. … providing it was all entered in a book and so on."

"If we wore jeans we'd be turned to stone"

Appearance was important for the Navy. Cadets were, and are, always smartly turned out, in the right rig for the right place and time. But there were just some rules … Michael Cochrane, there in the 1970s, was very amused by not being able to wear jeans:

> I remember being lined up on the ramps as … the new Captain, Captain Nicholas Hunt, very charismatic man, arrived. … Meryl his wife was wearing jeans and … we'd all been told that if we wore jeans we'd be turned to stone or something. … When we were marched off, we were taken quickly to a classroom and told 'just because the new Captain's wife wears jeans, does not make it acceptable for you to wear jeans.' … And then

The first female officers, spring 1973

Ronald Reagan became President of the United States, [and] he wore practically nothing but jeans. But [even] if he was Commander-in-Chief of the biggest armed forces in the world, no, we were not allowed to wear jeans. ... The system is always conservative.

"You were expected to be feminine"

In 1976, the Women's Royal Naval Service (WRNS) officer training was moved from Greenwich to Dartmouth where they formed Talbot Division. Female officer cadet training was to be fully integrated with men's in September 1990, but until then the WRNS was a separate service with increasing overlaps through 1980. Female cadets look back on their term at Dartmouth as so much history.

Carolyn Stait, Second Officer of Talbot Division in the 1980s, on the transition of the WRNS to Dartmouth:

> The moor exercise for us was called the Moor-Ex, that business of getting out and being physical on Dartmoor. ... I was later serving on the staff at Dartmouth ... under a splendid officer who'd been trained at Greenwich. As we were crossing Dartmoor, I asked her what the ... officer cadets at Greenwich had done that equated to our activity ... and she ... thought for a moment and said 'well, we would sometimes go for a walk through Greenwich Park.' That really establishes the difference between the two training patterns.

Nichola Winstanley, talking about the 1980s: "Your dress was checked. ... You would only wear trousers if they were part of a trouser suit. ... So you were expected to be feminine. ... [Now] away from work I live and die in trousers. ... It just wasn't done then. You've got to put it in context of what society was like then."

Women were fully integrated in the Navy after the end of this project. David Carpenter, 1970s, points out how much the Navy has changed:

> The next generation of submarines, the ones that are coming in as the Trident successor, will probably be constructed for dual manning. ... We might not have said so 40 years ago but,

actually, the more you go through life and the more I have had women on construction sites, women in the Navy, and now as cadets, the clearer it is that if you don't have women, you are excluding half the population. And if they have been picked by the Admiralty Interview Board, they are just as good as you.

Winstanley remembers: "WRNS ... did not go to sea. You just accepted that." But the limitations were not just the Navy regulations. For Winstanley, the greater opportunities open to women today are still limited by family:

If you want to be a nuclear physicist, if you want to train to be an astronaut, you know you can do it. There's nothing to hold you back. ... But society still expects us to be mums and to raise our children. ... And a chap that is prepared to do his fair share of raising the children and running the home is like gold dust. ... Society hasn't changed. Because whether we like it or not, biology [makes us] the nest-builders and child-rearers. ... Girls of today are faced with a lot of decisions and challenges that I never had to make. ... Those decisions were almost made for me. I had to leave the Navy and I had a baby.

"They will never serve at sea!"

When she joined the Naval Reserve and women did go to sea in 1993, Winstanley saw "a significant difference then in attitudes":

A RIB off the Dart, 1980s

And initially it was not necessarily positive. [Men had] definite ... suspicions [about womens'] roles on board the ships. There were two sorts: it would either be I need to protect you, or actually I'm just going to leave you stranded ... and if you think I'm coming to help you, Popeye, you've got another think coming. ... But that was exacerbated by the attitude of naval wives, who didn't like the thought of women serving at sea with their husbands. ... Interestingly they would be suspicious of us rather than their husbands.

What do the men say? That it's different, certainly. John Treacher, at the College in the 1930s, thought they would completely change going to war: "Take a missile on board, now, with girls on board. ... Missile goes through, kills 20 girls. It's all very different. It's not like anybody putting sails up … " But Paul Hart, 50 years later, saw the change as positive: "I work on … mixed manned ships and I have been in establishments where it's all mixed manned. There is a very different feel to it. I can't say better or worse – it's just different. And it works. It seems to work very well."

But it had to come. Michael Cochrane, talking about the 1970s: "Women weren't allowed at sea. I mean I was at Dartmouth when Mrs Thatcher was elected Prime Minister and there were still people saying 'well, we have a female as the Queen and a woman as Prime Minister, but they will *never* serve at sea!' A real nonsense."

"Everything has changed and nothing has changed"

But in a very fundamental way, training at the College was still the same for John Edge, 1980s:

Everything has changed and nothing has changed. … a lot of the values and underpinning reasons for the College, that leadership, development, management, communications, and the general positive attitude of [being] in the military, the chance that at some point you might be invited to put your life on the line in some form of conflict … is still there. All those shared values going back to Nelson's time … are still there.

Radar and telecommunications, 1980s

TRAINING

Prince Andrew, 1970s, summed up the impact of the training for himself: "Dartmouth training is relevant to getting you into the culture, the ethos, the tradition and the knowledge to be in the Navy."

"We were ground down"

What was it like? Cadets at the College over the 60 years after 1930 all remember intense activity, particularly in the first term, creating a sense of belonging to the Navy and their team.

Prince Andrew put it succinctly: "The first month, if I'm correct, was spent, as it were, having your brain removed and having a naval brain implanted." And Christopher Ayres, his contemporary, said:

> Dartmouth … breaks the shackles of being a civilian. I think that's why it was quite brutal to start with. To cut those bonds from home and mother … And cut away that dependence on the civilian life. You become part of the Navy in that 12–14 week period, which is quite a short period to create that belongingness.

"We were ground down to the lowest common denominator," Peter Booth said ten years earlier of that first term: "It didn't matter whether we were Indian, Malaysian, Australian, British, Scottish, Irish, Welsh. … Remorselessly, ruthlessly. On the parade ground, in the swimming bath, in the gym, on the sports field … Then I suppose we were built up. … [For] six weeks we got no leave at all."

The routine hardly changed over the 60 years after 1930 and former cadets remember every painful detail. John Forbes describes the 1930s:

> You got up at 6.30 and that was a performance. Everything was done to bells. You had so much time to have your cold shower, you had so much time to clean your teeth etcetera, you had so much time to get dressed. … You started at 6.30, had breakfast, then you had divisions on the parade ground. That was followed by instruction, academic or naval, until lunchtime. After lunch in the winter until tea was games … and you had to do something. Then after tea more instruction until supper. After supper another parade … and then more instruction until 9 o'clock and then

lights out at 9.30. Quite a long day, very little free time. On Wednesdays there wasn't instruction. In the summer the instruction took place before tea, then after tea there were games. That was the only difference between summer and winter.

In the 1980s, the system was virtually identical, except for the early morning exercises. Iain Cull has vivid memories: "Up at 5.30, early morning exercises 6–6.45, sevenish breakfast or scran, in 'Jack Speak' [naval idiom]. Then into lessons … ". For David Knight the dreaded early morning exercises in the 1970s involved:

> standing around on a hillside and watching a light through the falling rain in order to learn Morse code, or pulling a whaler up and down the river at astounding rates, or gym-swim combinations, or running … by which time you were ravenous. If you had managed to organise yourself sufficiently to get any breakfast, you ate everything. Still to this day food vaporises in front of me.

Jock Morrison recalls, in the 1950s, "endless hours on the parade ground, because that's the way you condition the mind," and, he adds, "to teach you how to love each other and how to hate the instructor, one or two of [whom] were not averse to giving you a good whack with a stick." It was a matter of "standing up straight, awake, alert, looking to the front, eyes not wobbling, cap on straight, clean cap, tie, everything … to shiny boots or shoes." Samson Mwathethe, one of two Kenyans in his term in the 1970s, remembers with pride escorting the colours on the parade ground, including on graduation day.

John Edge, in the 1980s, found it "a shock. … I had already done about three or four years of employment … so coming back … to sit in classrooms again, to be told what time to get up, what time to go to bed, what time to eat your meals, wasn't great. … But you're young and you get on with it."

Samson Mwathethe succeeded with "discipline and determination":

> When I started my training here … I thought maybe I would not finish the course. But I think with encouragement and determination, I [did] and was called to come back for the senior term. I think the determination is crucial. The encouragement that I got from my professor, and the divisional officer … helped to get me through.

"You have got to be dedicated"

Some floundered, like Patrick Harland in the 1940s:

> If you didn't quite make the grade, you were put down a term … a great pity because you then were not with your original comrades. … I was always terrified … and in my tenth-term report the headmaster said 'I fear he may have some difficulty in passing out'. My poor dear father was horrified that I had spent all this time at Dartmouth and I might not pass out. But it spurred me on and I

swotted a lot in my last term and I passed out with a second-class pass, about the middle of my term.

David Phillips did fail his first term in 1950, and his description resounds with sheer determination. He had joined as a naval rating at 18. "Scraped in," he said. His failure that first term "was a big disappointment":

> My parents actually came down. Dickinson was the Captain and I think my father talked to him. ... I wasn't surprised, because I could see from very early on that the pace of life ... and academic demands were about as much as I could cope with. But I was not fazed ... I have always felt that I was destined to become an Engineer Commander of a cruiser.

His success was down to pure grit:

> Nobody took me on one side and said 'oh, you poor chap, did you find it difficult?' The answer to that is, yes very difficult. It's the Royal Navy, we are not talking about the Girl Guides or public school. ... They thought about discharging me from the Navy ... [But] about half a dozen people stood up and said no, you can't kick Phillips out, he's going to make it in the end. And so I did. ... If you are going to do anything in life, you have got to be dedicated. And the one thing that I had, I think, perhaps more than most, was sheer dedication.

One way through

But some found ways to be more comfortable. David Price in the 1950s faced two problems: a Cadet Captain who insisted "you have to have a cold bath, and it's not just you walk in and have a cold bath, if you're late, you've got to do it twice" and a chest flat that could have icicles on the inside of the window. "However," he remembers, "within a week, I never had another cold bath." He volunteered to make the Cadet Captain's bunk:

> Looking after his bunk and his chest would take me no more than three minutes. So ... I had 17–18 minutes in my bunk every morning ... whilst the rest of them were running around, freezing cold. And I thought that was a pretty good bargain that.

Academics

Academic teaching at the College changed from offering a full secondary school syllabus in the 1930s–early 1950s to university-level and then post-graduate naval and technical courses. Anthony McCrum, coming from a prep school in the 1930s, recalls:

> The academic side in those days was absolutely first class. My ... happy memories of Dartmouth were the teachers. Particularly I had two inspiring teachers one in English, one in history. They left me with a love of poetry, and a love of history.

Each to his own. John Forbes, there at the same time, found "Maths and Science ... both brilliant", but:

> History and English ... were appalling. History was basically the Sea Kings of Britain, a collection of books written by an ex-tutor. If you wanted to know how they conducted wooden wars and fights that was great, but as far as I was concerned it wasn't history. English wasn't much better.

Forbes' contemporary, James Jungius, remembered that history master, "a man called Samson. He built a *trébuchet*; ... quite a big thing ... and he had a model castle over the blackboard [at which] he fired golf balls." William Melly, ten years later: "I never was taught by him, but they had pretty good fun in his classes, flinging stones and pebbles all round the room." And in the 1970s, the *trébuchet* gone, Christopher Ayres had much less fun: "On Saturday mornings, there was a complete period of history lessons ... which ritually ended the week. In fact I remember sitting, listening ... polishing me boots, as everyone else was. Either polishing their boots or asleep."

Jonathan Tod believed that teaching in the 1950s hadn't adapted to the arrival of older cadets: "The civilian lecturers had been there at the time people were joining as 13 or 16-year-olds and they had to be brought up to A-level standards. We were basically going in at A-level." And his contemporary, Joe Young felt: "As regards the ... school subjects ... I think that I went backwards when I was there."

Tod objected to the amount of mathematics the non-engineers had to learn in the 1950s. The engineers: "needed to keep their mathematical brains alive." But as for him, restricting:

> The academics to naval history and English – certainly learning how to write reports, records of incidents and that type of thing – would have been much more useful than teaching me all sorts of clever differentiation, integration, and spherical trigonometry. ... Throughout my naval career the most mathematics I've done is running the wardroom mineral account, counting the number of pigs up at Lossiemouth, or ... when I was the director of the defence programme, and I had £24 billion on my desk at the beginning of each year to share out.

A decade later, Andrew Craig found some use in all that maths:

> One of our mathematics lecturers was a Mr Cobbold, a lovely old guy. I think we probably almost gave him knobs on his ulcer because we weren't especially good at his [subject], and it was a religion to him ... But his hobby was how to beat the table at the casinos in France. So ... you could spend a whole mathematics lecture on [that], which was actually very useful practical knowledge. Far better than calculus.

Languages were important in the early days, when you could learn French, Spanish, German and Russian. "I suppose" said James Jungius, there in the 1930s: "because they reckoned we'd be travelling round the world." Jock Slater, in the 1950s, learnt Russian: "until I discovered that if I got any good I'd become the naval attaché in Moscow, so I gave up pretty quickly. ... But it's been very useful."

In the 1960s, David Lingard remembered the need for nuclear submariner engineers. Twenty years later, John Edge was learning: "the necessary tools to be able to understand the highly technical environment we operated in, nuclear submarines, aircraft carriers and state of the art jets."

"Monsieur de la Perelle, known as Deadly Peril"

Many cadets were inspired by the teaching at Dartmouth. Over 30 years later, they still remember names and details. William O'Brien, in his 90s, recalled whole phrases in French learnt in the 1930s:

> There was a very good French master. That was Mr Grenfell. Grenfell made us learn a particular recitation. When we were late we had to stand by his desk and say: "*Monsieur, je regrette infiniment d'arriver en retard. Jamais je ne ferai plus. J'ai fait tout le trajet à la course et maintenant je suis hors d'haleine. Et je veux me reposer un peu.*" ["Sir, please excuse me for arriving late. I won't do it again. I've run all the way and am now out of breath. And I would like to rest a little."] "*Bien,*" said Mr Grenfell. "*Asseyez-vous*".
> And that was it. That routine was gone through every time. Except with one cadet. One cadet, Leach, in my term was a grousy sort of person. ... He'd come in and Mr Grenfell would say "*Aha. De mauvaise humeur ce matin, Monsieur Leach? Uh?*" ["In a bad mood this morning, Mr Leach?"] and then he'd catch him by the hair above his temple here and give it a twist. That didn't do Leach's temper any good either. ... I came out of Dartmouth speaking quite good French. Entirely because of Grenfell.

Many cadets talked about Mark Sugden, not so good as a language teacher but poetic when playing rugby, and a good friend to many. John Forbes 1930s: "Mark Sugden had captained Ireland at rugger and therefore as far as I was concerned was a great hero. He taught French and Spanish not very well but he was super, and he and his wife befriended me. I had many cream teas with them and he also coached me in rugger."

William Melly remembered his tutor in the 1940s:

> Everybody had a tutor as in a university. ... My tutor was a man called Mr Whittall ... known as Weary Whitt, because he always looked a bit tired. But he had an MC from the First World War, when he threw his hat onto a hand grenade and sat on it and saved everybody around him. He was reputed to have half his behind made of tin. We never knew which half, and we would put drawing pins on the chair to see if they were bent when he got up. It may have been a complete fallacy anyway.

Melly also recalled:

[A] man called Monsieur de la Perelle, known as Deadly Peril ... who did wonderful drawings on the blackboard rather like Salvador Dali. He'd draw a head and he'd put a moustache on it and he'd put a bird on each end of the moustache. And you could learn Russian later on, as I did, and [be] taught by Count Sologub [in fact, Count Nicolas Sollohub], who'd been rescued from the Russian Revolution by his mother in a goods train.

Paul Rampling 1980s, has a PhD in oceanography that was inspired by Brian Parker:

... actually a nuclear engineer ... [who] taught oceanography. Maybe it's because he wasn't a professional in oceanography he made it sound really interesting and I just wanted to do that when I left the Navy. Also Eric Grove – he was teaching strategic studies – he was a famous historian. I think he's up in Hull University now. ... I came top in strategic studies when I was here.

There were always practical jokes, recalls Rupert Craven, 1930s:

Now, Mr Warner. A nice old boy, really. He taught physics. He had very big thick boots for some reason. And the science lecture rooms were sloped up and [there] were two terminals which you could connect power to for various electric experiments.

Picket boats were mentioned by many; this recent photograph will stimulate memories

Well of course, it was natural, wasn't it, to connect a little power to them because Mr Warner had the habit of swinging up on them when he spoke.

"You have to have the basic skills"

Cadets remember basic naval training in the classroom, learning on great big models, and on boats on the river. Like so many others, Peter Booth liked the river in the 1960s, but he preferred the power boats. He wished he had kept his river logs because of "the number of times I lied about what I had done to get away." He didn't like sailing:

You started off learning to sail what was called a Royal Navy Sailing Association Dinghy, which was a small dinghy but very heavy. If you capsized it, it was a devil of a job to get up. ... Rigging the boat to start off with, getting the sails ready and up, then unrigging it at the end of the day – pain in the arse that was … . Then we sailed in the whalers, the cutters and the yachts …sometimes just a day out and sometimes for a weekend. I quite enjoyed that in the fairly calm weather but I didn't enjoy it very much on the rougher weather. So I loved the power boats, with the picket boats and the fast motor boats. And then there was a strange one called the Kitchen Rudder boat, a pinnace with a different way of operating the rudder and the propeller. That took a little bit of skill [and] … practice to handle properly. But that was good fun.

Jock Slater, in the 1950s, had memories of seasickness and "character-forming" episodes on the platform of the navigation mast with the sea rolling and the mast "going quite something." And at the same time Jock Morrison recalled: "It was quite tough, hands frozen to this large piece of wood, being shouted at by a manic Australian midshipman who wanted to go around the next buoy, not this one, that one, old Bluey."

John Lippiet, 1960s, was succinct about his priorities: forget about polishing boots "the bullshit end of the training", but remember the seamanship and the development of the seaman's eye:

In navigation now everyone's used to satnavs and looking at an electronic chart and so on. … I have done a lot of very basic navigation and charting, and then astronavigation … to be able to do star sights. … [But] all these wonderful gadgets of today will fail and in war they may completely, deliberately fail, and there will be many, many people who will be lost at sea … . You have to have the basic skills.

He described how he needed his Morse:

I didn't think I'd ever need Morse, but as a sub-lieutenant in my first ship, in the middle of the night I was put on board a yacht that was sinking and towed it back in very rough weather. My radio gave up within seconds but I had a Pusser's torch, and I knew enough Morse to flash to the frigate towing me … to slow down. … I was very thankful then to be able to do Morse.

Michael Fulford-Dobson in the 1940s: "I did a lot of rowing, a lot of sailing and, although I didn't become a specialist, I've always taken a particular pride and enjoyment in navigation. … I loved [to say] 'at 9:06, the day after tomorrow, we'll go underneath the Forth Bridge'. One took great pride in actually achieving that."

Anthony McCrum's seamanship training was tested by his later experiences during the war on minesweepers, one being *HMS Skipjack* that was sunk at Dunkirk, and destroyers. He found his teaching wanting. First, his teachers were officers, not trained teachers, and "all the seamanship training was done on funny little models which bore no relation to the size of the things at … sea." McCrum goes on:

Investigating ship stability and damage control, 1987

During the four years I was at Dartmouth we never actually sailed in an HM ship. ... I passed out bottom in seamanship. When I passed out of the cadet training cruiser I got the seamanship prize. And that was the difference between sitting in model rooms and actually doing it. ... I always remembered that when I was training people later on in life. You need the reality. You don't want little models.

"If somebody comes at you with a knife ... "

Julian Loring, who joined the College in 1947, remembers the physical training instructors from the Royal Marines:

In the last term ... we had unarmed combat lessons. We weren't exactly taught how to kill somebody with one blow. But we were told what to do. If somebody comes at you with a knife over the head, you don't bother too much because he doesn't know what he's doing. [But] if someone comes at you with the knife going upwards then he does know what he's doing. If he comes at you throwing the knife from one hand to the other then he certainly knows what he's doing and all you can do is turn tail and run. ... If somebody comes up behind you and tries to strangle you, grab hold of his little fingers and break them. They don't like that. And if you are a lady and somebody does this and you're wearing heels, bring one up and stamp on his foot because you will put down a force of about quarter of a ton and he won't like that either. Useful? Yes.

Many former cadets talked about the petty officers with affection. "We had lovely ... chief petty officers who were retired chiefs or petty officers and very much the sort of father figure who tried to keep a discreet eye on what we were doing and I think on the whole did it very well," says Loring. His contemporary William Melly still remembers their special language: the nicknames, Spud Murphy, Potts the painter and Chippy the carpenter, Holy Commotion for Holy Communion, the "Matthew Walker [hitch] used for becketts and buckets" when the Navy had long given up canvas buckets and Chief Petty Officer Marks who said "now today we're going to do a double Matthew Walker for bigger becketts for better buckets."

Female officer training. Drawing by Mandy Shepherd

Some of the training of the WRNS officers was badly outdated. Karen Peach was the First Officer WRNS in 1986–88 (equivalent to a Lieutenant Commander) when Talbot Division had some 16–26 WRNS under training:

> At this stage, the girls were still limited as to what jobs they would do when they left. Most of them were still secretarial or administrative jobs. A few were being taken as instructor officers … Hence a lot of the actual training was on how to fill in forms, or how to run a female division [with only] naval history and international affairs on the academic side … But I was slightly perturbed [to find] that they still … had make-up lectures. After a couple of months of this, I said 'no, no, no, this isn't what training should be, they're training to be officers, not training to be fashion models.' And similarly there was … the Pauline Doyle trophy, presented to the girl who kept her femininity while parading round the parade ground. Now if anything was antiquated, it was that I'm afraid.

Sports were good

Everyone had to do sport daily, not a burden for most cadets who had joined the Navy because they were physically active and enjoyed the outdoor life. Depending on the era, there was a tremendous range to choose from, with an emphasis on competitive games.

Anthony McCrum, 1930s: "The College was cleared after lunch and we all had to be in sports rig and we all had to do something. In winter hockey, rugby, cross country running. And you weren't allowed back in the College until tea time at four."

There was "a log", recalled his contemporary William O'Brien, "and you had to record your log. And for example, a run to Black Cottage which was about three miles up the road above Dartmouth, counted as a full log. A game of squash was only half a log, so we had to find another bit of exercise [to complete] … the log every day. You were monitored even in your exercise." Many cadets record fixing their logs.

"Team games were everything"

Rugby was always a popular winter sport. In the 1950s, Dartmouth was playing "top class rugby", said David Wixon, with internationals among the cadets and the instructors:

> I played a lot of rugby, playing for the Navy and Devon when I was at Manadon [post Dartmouth], which was a highlight of my naval career. When I was getting married to my first wife ... apparently I said [to my best man] 'this is almost as good as playing at Twickenham.' ... We had three or four internationals in our side, and [the] priority was national teams, counties and the services in that order. So it was big stuff in those days. [At Dartmouth] we had Alan Meredith, an instructor commander who was a Welsh cap. And we had the very famous Mark Sugden, who was a scrum half for Ireland. And if any young cadet had an Irish element in his ancestry, they had even more interest from Mark. ... I was very fond of Mark Sugden.

Mark Sugden. Photograph Adrian Lloyd-Edwards

O'Brien, another rugby player, remembered Sugden 20 years earlier: "He played such good rugger. And he played it in such a very nice way; such a perfect temperament. ... It was real poetry to watch him. ... He could throw the ball coming out of the scrum and pass it the whole length of the three-quarter line into the other wing three-quarter's tummy."

O'Brien enjoyed the symbols of success: "[When] you became a member of the first 15 you put on your blazer the Naval crown and 'First 15, 1934 or 1935' or whatever it was. If you did it two years, you put '1934-1935'. And you were then called an 'adds date'. Quite a distinction. 'He's an adds date because he's a big chap.' And I was an 'adds date' for rugby."

A number of cadets from the 1940s–early 1950s remember competition between the Darts, the 13-year-olds (all those public schoolboys), and the older entries, such as the Benbows, or Special Entries (who couldn't march), spilling over into sports. Neil Blair, in the 1950s, has fond memories of being on "the first Benbow team to beat the Darts at rugby." Michael Fulford-Dobson in the 1940s, saw a class element in it: "It wasn't until probably you got to being a midshipman that the Darts and the Benbows started to be indistinguishable from each other and there was a lot of rivalry as you can imagine. All these chaps coming from all these smart public schools."

Individualism

Despite the emphasis on team games, many took up individual sports, such as running or swimming. Prince Andrew, in the 1970s, "used to run in full battle order up that blasted hill from the bottom all the way to the top and I tell you what, there aren't many people who could do that, then or now! And I used to do it in full fighting order."

Andrew Craig, in the 1960s, took advantage of the "extra-curricular activities that Dartmouth had to offer, which were numerous and wonderful" to get a private pilot's licence to fly Tiger Moths. This led to "[what] seemed to me a very good idea … to fly back over the College and at very low level down the river … because it was a nice sunny day. And because I was really very unversed in these things, I did a couple of passes". But at the College they took the side number of the plane and when he got back to Dartmouth. "All aviators," he was told, "do this once in their career. You have now had your one and only chance to do a bit of freebie low flying. Do not ever do that again."

Craig never did it again:

> That drilled itself into my brain very deeply indeed. Having gone on to be a proper aviator in my later career, I was very wary about unauthorised and ridiculous low flying. … Young pilots will do silly things, you can wring their neck for doing them, but it's probably not going to serve any purpose. Just scare the hell out of them and they probably won't do it again.

Fencing was another option and Mark Barton, in the 1980s, remembers wanting to fence, surprisingly not because of the WRNS: "The senior who was teaching it spent most of his time trying to impress the young WRNS. … Fortunately a group of fencers … realised that I was actually trying to properly learn … and taught me … It was all done on the quarterdeck, a lovely setting."

And some cadets chose a sport to maximise the quiet life. David Price found out that if he did boxing in the 1950s, he could reduce his games time from 2 hours to 30 minutes:

> Every afternoon … the College is cleared from 1400 to 1600. … Everybody has to be outside, doing something. Except the boxing clique. Because … if you are in the boxing clique you're doing these exercises, like skipping in boots and running and sparring. For young boys this is really tremendous exercise and therefore they need to go and rest afterwards. … So I volunteer for the boxing clique and I turn up in the afternoons and have my half hour of running around in boots. I then go back into the College [to lie] on my bunk.

Ballroom dancing meant cadets danced with each other in the early decades

LEISURE

Former cadets remember many good times, despite the pressure – this comes through across the decades and across all memories. Judy Faulkner, one of the early women cadets in the 1970s: "So what made it work? There was such good balance between really pushing yourself and hard work, wonderful environment and great fun. Lots and lots of laughs."

"We couldn't go into Dartmouth"
Going into town, or "ashore", in the early days, was forbidden. To Adrian Holloway's regret in the 1930s: "We were very sorry we couldn't go into Dartmouth. It's a pretty little town, and I don't know whether they were afraid we might get up to some mischief." Except, said Duncan Knight, at the same time, if, despite wartime restrictions, parents came and took cadets out for a whole day: "We were absolutely imprisoned. Except on this one whole holiday … we were released at 8 o'clock, so you could go and have breakfast with your parents and be with them all day … They could actually take you to a town."

But by the 1950s, 18-year-olds were joining and restrictions eased. Neil Blair, a Special Entry from South Africa, remembers: "After three weeks we inevitably ended up at the Floating Bridge pub by the higher ferry [with] probably half a dozen of the rugger side." And "the Floaters" was where Joe Young, also 1950s, first learnt to drink: "I had to ask what to order when I first went in. It was part of the Navy life. And we would pop next door for double egg and chips from the kind ladies who ran the Midships café. Cost one and eight pence, double eggs and chips, it was fantastic."

A far cry from Knight's sense of being imprisoned, Michael Cochrane, in the 1970s, has colourful memories of a sortie downtown that left a permanent mark on the College landscape:

I had a car at Dartmouth. I had great fun with that. It was a tiny little Citroën with the tiniest engine, and one of my chums had a very fast MG sports car. ... We had a bet that I could race to this pub in Dartmouth before him. And it was all [about] who could get to the first corner first. And the little Citroën had very springy suspension and big huge wheels, and I just drove straight down over the golf course [then between the College building and the front gates], crashed into a bush, bit awkward, but that wasn't going to stop me because I had a bet, no points for coming second. And I got to the pub before him. He was amazed. The Commander of the College was fairly amazed. Asked me why I did it, well I said I was having a race. He wasn't very pleased with that. But he … was reasonably sympathetic. … On the [next] mess bill … I had to pay £8 for a bush.

Lovely Sundays

Anthony McCrum, 1930s: "On Sundays we were allowed to go to a farm and … three or four friends would book a farm for the term. And we would take our gramophone and our records and we would have a cream tea and listen to Bye bye blackbird and [the] latest tunes of the day."

You had to pay, Duncan Knight remembered:

> You could buy a damn good cream tea with boiled egg and everything else, if you could pay. … My pay was a shilling a week so obviously we couldn't do it on that, so hopefully your parents will have pressed a half crown or two into your hands, although they were told not to. … The alternative was for the parents to write direct to the farm … sending a ten-shilling note or something saying 'feed my son up.' And so if you knew somebody whose father was doing that, that was a very good move indeed.

Farms presented opportunities that were later perhaps regretted. Adrian Holloway, 1930s, recalled official cuts being administered to "this chap [who] … was caught in a rather amatory embrace with the farmer's daughter."

Ballroom dancing

Dancing at Dartmouth mirrored the shifts in social mores after the 1930s. By the 1970s, dancing lessons were an opportunity to get to know the WRNS, but cadets from the 1930s-early 60s still remember mostly dancing with each other. Dancing, the Navy believed, was essential for an officer. Duncan Knight, 1930s felt that dancing "stood us all in very good stead":

> When I [was] a midshipman in South Africa … we held *thés dansants* … dancing with drinks and tea … . My captain … Bob Burnett, a famous Admiral in the war and very terrifying to a midshipman, would … if he saw ladies sitting out, call over a midshipman, 'come here now and go and look after that lady there.' … So we needed to know … the proper dances.

"The dancing class was quite simple," said David Price, of the 1950s:

> You went into the quarterdeck. You lined up, tallest at one end and [shortest] at the other. The first person, the tallest, is the man, and the next one down is the girl. Peter Tyrell was slightly taller than I, he was the man and I was his dancing partner. Now I can do most fantastic fantails,

fishtails, whirls, swirls and the waltz and the quickstep. But I don't know the rumba and samba, because by that time we'd managed to get behind the pillars into a classroom and out through the window and be sitting on the grass near what used to be the art block.

And they remembered the dancing teachers – Joe Young in the 1950s had Miss Veale:

A very, very persistent lady. The worst thing that could happen to you was, if you were so bad, she'd dance with you. So there was a terrific incentive to avoid that. ... My partner was a chap called Peter Hoskins, and I used to call him Hot Lips Hoskins. This great hairy thing, he was. It was just fun really. ... But you couldn't horse around too much, because otherwise you might have to dance with Miss Veale.

But Knight trumps it all with his memories of cadets dancing with the future Edward VIII, who would often visit the College. In a dance called the Paul Jones, "when the music stopped you had to dance with the person opposite you. ... So somebody ended up opposite him. I never did, but he could say I danced with the Prince of Wales, whereas most people could [only] say my sister danced with somebody who danced with the Prince of Wales three times removed."

There were always a few girls; the Captain in the 1940s had daughters. One, Pansy, caused the expulsion of one cadet. But Richard Hill recalled that "we all shied away from them, we would sooner dance with each other, not for sexual reasons but because we were shy." Girls came to the end-of-training dance at the College, and Peter Booth remembers in the 1960s that the formidable Gladys Veale had "Saturday hops" in Kingswear – with girls: "But we had to do ballroom dancing until the last dance when it was a bit of a snog and it was a bit slow. But that was the only concession Gladys allowed."

Times moved on and ballroom dancing with boys at the College ceased. Well before it did, Rolfe Monteith, a Special Entry from Canada in the 1940s, was mystified:

To the North American, this was unbelievable! Suddenly a message was received ... on the grapevine 'oh, there's going to be a dance this evening'. And we Canadians, we thought 'oh my God, we'd better go and sound this out'. We arrived there and said 'where are the ... girls?' 'There are none.' 'There are none?' 'No, you dance with each other.' You ... just couldn't credit it today. [Dancing] was huge learning curve for the Canadians. I felt for most of them.

And then came the WRNS. When Christopher Ayres joined in the 1970s:

We had the first intake of WRNS officers. ... Not many. And each division had a couple ... attached to it. A chit went round saying, anybody interested

Monarchs and Mariners, Jubilee pageant 1977

in dancing, 'a good skill to learn', blah blah blah. Some of us recognised, 'ah, there will be WRNS officers doing this as well'. An opportunity to mix with the WRNS was good. So I did learn to dance.

Hobbies and fun

Cadets with particular talents found time for them. Julian Loring in the 1940s was a radio enthusiast:

We had a radio … so we could get the lunch-time cricket scores … The radio club [included] quite a distinguished physics master, John Runge, who was one of the earlier amateur radio enthusiasts. … One of our number actually made a television using a radar scope, 6 inches it was, but it worked. We were all most impressed. Also very impressed with American radio equipment, which was incredibly neat and pretty and well put together, and all shiny and aluminium whereas ours – oh dear! oh dear! Great hefty thing with huge great batteries.

Patrick Harland played the violin in the 1940s: "In my last term, I won the Whitworth Memorial Prize for music." And he recalls "a marvellous teacher when … we were at Eaton Hall, who'd been leader of the Hallé Orchestra, Jimmy Matthews. … He always used to call me 'my dear old boy'. … A parishioner of my father's in Chelsea gave him a violin for me. It was a … 1750-ish violin … had it all my life and it accompanied me whenever I joined a ship."

Others found acting niches. Jolyon Waterfield in the 1940s was "more or less bludgeoned … to join the chorus of The Gondoliers". For Stephen Daltrey in the 1970s acting was a chance to shine:

I was never particularly sporty and I wasn't doing so well academically either. … But I took the lead role in the College play, called Charlie's Aunt. … I was able to mix then with the staff officers and their wives and get a very different view of the College and build relationships etc. Fond memories of that. It was the best way I could express myself fundamentally.

Judy Faulkner, one of the early WRNS in the 1970s, managed, in her one term at Dartmouth, to cram in quite a bit:

> We had parties. One particular one ... was a 'what you were wearing when the ship went down' party, so there were some fairly scantily dressed men and women at that. ... I did choir so in the build-up to Christmas we had the most wonderful carol concert, singing carols that I'd never heard of, but were just beautiful. ... I did fencing and ... beagle walking, which was a bizarre activity. ... Our course did a review for Christmas, which was hilarious, taking off all the instructors.

Prince Andrew remembers a traditional royal exploit in the 1970s – signing the ceiling of the wardroom:

> The Prince of Wales had signed it. They had then painted the ceiling and just before I came they left a hole [for me]. ... It was about the last evening's mess dinner. ... We just took over the wardroom and [we made a human tower] with three layers to get to the top and I just managed to get the signature in before it collapsed in a heap.

Cycling Club, 1980s

ENFORCING THE RULES

"You can't have any slackness"
All former cadets remembered the pressure of their time at Dartmouth – see the section on training. They believed that all that drilling and obeying rules at the double built self-discipline, and that learning self-discipline was an essential preparation for going to sea.

Anthony McCrum, 1930s: "It undoubtedly did prepare one for a disciplined service. If you run a ship it's got to be spot on. You can't have any slackness; you can't have anyone not doing their job properly. A ship is a dangerous place particularly in bad weather." And Michael Cochrane, 1970s: "You just needed to get on and do it. If it's your job to have a tidy cabin, then have a tidy cabin. If it's your job to hand in paperwork on time, then hand it in on time. It stops that slackness of mind." James Jungius remembers of the 1930s: "There was a terrific emphasis … on punctuality. If you were told to do something at 4 o'clock you didn't do it at 3.59. You did it at 4 o'clock."

And self-discipline is essential to leadership. "Why?" asked Andrew Craig, 1960s: "Because you are an officer and have got a bunch of sailors who are your responsibility. … It gets back to this old business which Dartmouth was very good at. If you have men under your command you really have to lead by example … whether that's in the trivial things like keeping your kit neat, or whether it's in the more advanced things."

The many rules to do with personal tidiness were also because ships were small, and spaces for personal possessions very restricted. "You go to sea," says Craig, "you have responsibility for a division of 30 sailors … who have a very small kit locker in which to keep their kit, and a fairly rigid way of stowing it. … If you can't do it yourself, you can't really lean on your sailors and expect them to do it."

Cochrane recalls how the rule was learnt: "There were inspections every night on your room and your kit had to be laid out absolutely perfectly. … It was a way of teaching you to live in a confined space … and that's as relevant now as it was then."

The beatings, the cuts and the strafes
The penalties for not keeping to the rules evolved. In the early decades, corporal punishment featured, as it did in other schools and in society generally, and all those early cadets had clear memories of

Rounds, checking cabins, clothes and boots, mid-1980s

it. If they did not suffer themselves, they certainly remembered it happening to others.

The first level were the ticks – the records of infractions – that led to the beatings. William O'Brien, 1930s: "You doubled [ran] past all senior gunrooms. If you didn't and you were caught it was four ticks in the book and four cuts on the bottom. … You saluted every officer and every master you saw in the corridors, no matter if you had saluted him three times in the past hour. … That meant you always had to have your cap on at all times of day. Took it off in the classroom, put it on after."

William Melly remembers being caught out at Eaton Hall in the 1940s:

> Every night were rounds in the huts. And we had a marvellous old boy [who was] Commander of the College called Weir, who'd been called back. And he had a flippin' dog which had a nose like a hound, and if there was a bun or something under the chest where it shouldn't be, he'd bring it out and drop it at his master's feet. Aaah! … Yep. You might get a beating for having a bun under your chest.

So much for beating. Then, said McCrum:

> [We had] official cuts, if it was a serious offence. In the gymnasium. And the whole term is marched up there. The … victim, is strapped to the box horse; ankles and wrists strapped down. And then the physical training instructor, considered a worthy wielder of the cane, carried out the beating. … The term was turned about so we couldn't see but we could hear if he screamed. … If he screamed we would consider he was bit of a wimp. And then we turned about again and he joined up with the term and we all doubled away.

Rodney Agar's memory of official cuts in the 1940s highlights the difference between Dartmouth and Eaton Hall in cadets' lives during the war: "We had two in our term beaten with official cuts. … They had climbed the wall into the Duke of Westminster's garden and helped themselves to some of his peaches."

Richard Hill, 1940s, records the case of the Captain's daughter: "One [cadet] was … famous for his escapades with [Pansy], the Captain's daughter. He got official cuts and got chucked out of the College in the end for his attention to Pansy." Tom

Potts, a contemporary, recalls: "one of the senior cadets took a swing at one of the chief cadet captains … who he didn't get on with and official cuts were delivered … "

Then there were strafes, punishments meted out to the whole term for failings by the entire group or just individuals. It was all part of team building; everyone had an interest in making sure every member would stay out of trouble.

Duncan Knight, 1930s, recalls that "if the cadet captains or term officer decided the whole term was below standard, and it could easily happen if on parade your term didn't do well, the term strafe would be ordered." A strafe could also be ordered if individual cadets "were deemed to have done the wrong thing with their rifles … " He remembers: "they were absolute hell. For certain they involved running down to Sandquay, about 300 steps to the bottom, I believe, and back up again, and goodness knows how many bunny hops and press ups. They were pretty grim."

"A haircut. And then another haircut"

As the new entries of officer cadets became older and society changed, corporal punishment disappeared. Jonathan Tod, at the College in the 1950s, when boys were starting to have long hair:

> The first penalty was to get a haircut. And then be sent away to get another haircut because your first haircut wasn't good enough. But then there was also the instant penalties, running round the

Extra exercise in the gym, 1987

ramps at the College … classes for people who were backward in [something] … perhaps Morse code or flags or swimming … which meant that you got up early. Then they [could stop] … your leave, so you weren't allowed to go ashore. In your first six weeks … you weren't allowed to go ashore anyway, which meant we saved up all our money for a really good run ashore on the first night we were allowed out. But I had discovered at that stage that if you had a bag of old golf clubs, you could claim you were going out to play golf. You were allowed to go out and play golf, although you weren't allowed to go out on leave.

Peter Booth recorded of the 1960s:

> Punishments were called ROB, required on board. There were three different levels, Alpha, Bravo and

Charlie. Alpha was the simple one, you just got your leave stopped and you had to report to the Duty Officer at certain times during the day. ROB Charlie was the bugger. You had to get up half an hour early, you did a lot more physical work, you got no free time at 'stand easy' in the middle of the morning [or] … at lunchtime. You had to do extra parade training. You had to do things like parade training with a rifle and run round the ramps with the rifle above your head. … [double] up and down to Sandquay … So physically you were punished quite hard. Mentally you got about an hour's rest in the evening when you had to clean charts. … Bravo … was somewhere in between.

"Our swearing ability increased a hundred-fold"

"Was I shouted at?" Christopher Ayres, remembering the 1970s:

In those days, you took orders by the tone of voice. And a lot of the instructors … used the power of command in the loudness of their voice. Particularly on the parade ground, because you have to make your voice heard. A raft of very blue words was used, so our swearing ability increased a hundred-fold in those six months. … The idea was, you were given a task, and [according to] the tone of the voice, you jumped to it and got on with it.

People inevitably dwelt on the penalty they hated most. Many had to do with folding those clothes. David Phillips in the 1950s:

The worst thing that ever happened was that if you used any of your kit to go and play games it all had to be folded back exactly as it was before you took it out. I can remember coming back from something or other like boating on the river, and … finding practically all my kit chucked on the deck because it wasn't folded properly.

And John Madgwick, 1960s, recalls:

Some of the … third-year people would institute a rig-changing punishment. It meant you would arrive in one particular rig and go away and change into something else and go through a cycle from sports rig to evening wear to river wear to daily wear. This was boring in itself, but it meant that one's locker was then a complete mess at the end of it all and had to be put back together neatly and exactly in time for evening rounds that night. That was probably the most arduous punishment.

Jock Morrison, there in the 1950s, could have given them some advice: "The cadets' ploy was to use the laundry basket a lot. All usable clothing was kept in the laundry basket, and the drawers were never touched, just dusted sometimes."

The arrival of the women

Women arrived in the College in the 1970s. Understandably, since women were not being trained to go to sea, Carolyn Stait, on the third course for WRNS at the College, recorded that the separation of the genders held in discipline as well as in most other things: "I don't think the men were very into wanting to discipline the women. ... [They] would always just hand it over to the divisional staff in Talbot Division and leave them to mete out whatever they thought was appropriate."

"Lots of relationships happened here at the College"

Women arriving opened whole new territories for discipline. Nichola Winstanley, 1980s, when asked whether there were love interests, replied:

> Yes, very much so. In fact I met my first husband whilst we were here ... When we got together at the end of my term here, I was found in his cabin and that was not allowed. And so the two of us were both put on stoppage of leave ... about 10 or 12 days before the end of term. My parents were coming down and I couldn't go ashore to see them ... Actually ... [I] could have been dismissed from the College. I certainly knew of previous WRNS officer cadets found with partners or boyfriends [who were] removed. So I was very worried that that was going to happen to me.

Did it work?: "You're a bit of a wet; you haven't been beaten yet"

That early corporal punishment encouraged a counter-productive culture. Anthony McCrum, 1930s, always remembers his third term:

Some of my chums would say McCrum you're a bit of a wet; you haven't been beaten yet. I hadn't and I got quite worried. They kept saying 'You're not a real man'. So I started a sort of campaign of trying to get beaten, and leaving my clothes around, being late for class. No one seemed to notice. I left more things around, I arrived later for class. There were various petty things you could do and eventually the great day came. We were always beaten in the evenings. And if the light was left on in the landing outside the dormitory we could see because we had glass in the doors. And on this night, the light was on. 'McCrum turn out'. I thought at last I've done it! And so then I had my three cuts and then of course it was compulsory in the morning to show your bum to the whole term. To show that you had been caned properly. What a carry on!

Jolyon Waterfield reported how, ten years later, cadets cut notches in their hairbrushes for every stroke of the cane:

> And of course, the guy that had notches all the way round his hairbrush and needed another ... was really the hero. ... Precisely what corporal punishment was designed to discourage. So in that respect corporal punishment failed and probably it's one of the reasons why it no longer applies in schools today. Quite rightly too. But corporal punishment was part of our life and accepted on the chin.

Many cadets thought all the rules and the drilling excessive. Michael Cochrane, 1970s, said "it was ridiculous really, it was unnecessarily high standards." And McCrum, although he saw the sense of discipline, still, in his 90s, thought it over the top:

> You can't teach discipline. ... If you questioned [parade drills], which I did ... you were told this was to ensure that you instantly obeyed an order. If you're taught how to stand, come to attention, stand at ease, or shoulder arms properly, then you will always be responsive to orders. I thought I could do all that in about three months. But we spent hours on the parade ground ...

For Paul Hart, in the 1980s, who was older and had already been in the Army, discipline simply didn't work:

> Having spent many hours in the crash superman position when I was on commando course, which incidentally involved putting your forehead on the ground with your feet on the ground then putting your hands behind your back so you were bent double, with nothing between your head and the concrete. I was pretty impervious to the discipline that Dartmouth offered which was somebody standing in front of me and shouting. It just washed over me.

And was the power to punish abused? Most cadets remember there was a fine line. William O'Brien,

Right rig at the right time – collecting pocket money in the 1940s

1930s: "The [senior cadets who] made sure you were thrashed ... had a lot of power. ... And it wasn't abused ... very much. But occasionally it was. When a cadet captain thought a cadet ought to be thrashed, he made sure he did something wrong and he'd put a tick in the book. He'd invent it all, which he could easily do. Your tie's crooked. Tick. Four ticks and you got beaten." Jock Morrison, 1950s: "A parade officer [gave] me one day's punishment for something stupid like having a hand folded incorrectly. And then when I said 'why?' He said 'three days punishment because you're Scottish.'"

Just get it right

There were always those who took rules and penalties as part of life. David Carpenter at the College in the 1970s didn't really remember them:

> You could have extra work or drill, a bit like detention at school really. You were found some small irksome task to perform, polishing the guns, if you had been late, or adrift, or scruffy. There wasn't much else. There was no drinking, [people were] unlikely to be mutinous, so it almost didn't arise really. It was just part of being in that establishment.

And Jonathan Tod, 1950s, didn't see what the problem was: "The discipline side in fact was no different from a public school … You basically did what you were told. And you turned up in the right rig at the right time."

John Lippiett, ten years later, found enforcing discipline quite logical: "It taught you method, it taught you self-discipline. … And if you got it wrong, you suffered more, so the way to ease the suffering was to get it right. That's no bad way of training."

The pinch of salt: "As long as your prank didn't go too wrong … you would get away with it"

David Knight in the 1970s emphasised the importance of good humour with the discipline:

> The combination of discipline and humour … is very important. It's very important in a ship at sea, in an air squadron, or a submarine or [anywhere]. You have got to have discipline, but you have also got to have humour so that people can give what they have to give wholeheartedly and enjoy the process. Otherwise you won't retain your officers and ratings.

Former cadets quote many examples of how the College used judgement in applying the rules. A blind eye was turned when David Price brought a motorcycle in his last term as a cadet in the 1950s:

> At that time vehicles in the College owned by cadets were certainly frowned upon. I'm not sure if it was legal, but certainly as far as I was aware no other cadets had cars. So when I arrived with my motorbike I left it at Sandquay. … This motorcycle gave me my freedom. … Needless to say … when I had an accident the first person who came by in his car was the Captain of the College. He opened his car window … and said, 'Are you alright Price?' I said, 'Yes Sir, just had a little accident.' He said, 'OK, well if there are any problems just ring the College.' I said, 'Alright Sir, goodnight.'

Mark Barton in the 1980s remembered the same tolerance of high spirits:

> If you got caught you'd get punished. But you got the impression that [breaking the rules] was sort of half approved of. … There were lots of things you couldn't fail, also lots of things that if you failed you would get removed. But … you could do wrong things and get the punishment, [yet] it was almost seen as having character. … So as long as your prank didn't go too wrong, you didn't actually break anything or break anything too seriously, then you would get away with it. It was just seen as high spirits. And that seemed to be … tolerated.

What did the non-British cadets think of the tolerance of some rule-breaking? Andrew Craig, an Australian, 1960s, recalls:

> Nobody beat us up, but we were expected to toe the line and play the game according to the rules. And … shall we say, benign transgressions were accepted. But if you were stupid about it, you got a fairly smart and well deserved whack under the ear. I did feel sorry for some of the other nationalities there. For the Australians or New Zealanders it was all pretty straightforward but [hardly for] … the Kenyans … Malaysians and Singaporeans and indeed the souls from Ghana and even Ethiopia. Those poor folk I think went through their year at Dartmouth with their eyes wide open, wondering [why] on earth these strange people conducted themselves in the way they did.

"You weren't giving up your personality but you were joining a club"

Terry Jane, 1960s, believed: "Basic training is still terrible for everybody in the services nowadays, because it's so alien to anything that they've come across." But the point was to create a Navy:

> At the time you felt you were just being forced to do very strange physical things that seemed to have no point in them, that you had no time to yourself and you were rushing around. Looking back on it, you realise that they were giving you a sense of discipline, giving you a sense of pride in your appearance and making you understand that by conforming you weren't giving up your personality but you were joining a club.

LEADERSHIP

Born leaders?: "If you have the initial qualities you'll make a good officer"

Many cadets commented on the balance of natural skills for leadership – they often referred to people in their intake who were destined to go far – and the capacity to learn them. The College itself implicitly confirmed the need for both by focussing the initial selection process on identifying leadership potential.

"Were we being made into young Nelsons?" asked Christopher Ayres, 1970s: "No, we were being made into competent officers. There were some clearly within our group … who, you could tell, were going to go a long way. But for the bulk of us, it was get on the treadmill, work our way through the system and learn as much as we could to do our best."

Iain Cull, 1980s, remembers:

> There was this [view of] nature over nurture … and therefore you were a leader before you joined. I think we have wised up and [believe that] actually you can develop leadership. OK you have to have the potential. … [But we have gone from when] officers were born into this role, to realising that actually they just have to have the talent and the skill-set that can be developed.

David Lingard, 1960s, believed a leader had to have a technical understanding of the job in hand:

> That may sound basic but actually there is a tendency to think that you can provide a leader who doesn't know a damn thing about the job he is actually trying to do. I don't believe that … be you an Executive Officer driving a ship as a Captain, or an Engineer looking after your engines or your weapons systems, you need that technical knowledge … . You are then able to achieve a rapport with your staff and get the best out of them.

An enduring training model: "Leadership was being drawn out of you"

How did the College teach leadership – the fine art of getting people to do things they didn't particularly want to do? A consistent model was applied across the 60 years, that is clear. But many ex-cadets remember leadership being so embedded

Rope work. Drawing by Mandy Shepherd

in College routines that they were hardly aware of it being explicitly taught. Prince Andrew, 1970s, recalls "leadership was being drawn out of you, just by experiencing the day-to-day routine. ... The time we spent on the river in picket boats ... was actually learning how to act as a crew." And 40 years earlier Derek Willan said: "Being able to take charge of a ship's company ... was inbred as a result of my time at Dartmouth. It was not so much the formal teaching as what you were doing. The drills, that sort of thing, were all part of the teaching."

Some models of classroom teaching were mentioned. John Lippiet recalls the "Adair approach" in the 1960s: "If I got it right, it was: task, individual, team, looking at each and looking at the relationships between each."

Andrew Craig, 1960s, recalls:

You got lectures on leadership and how you need to lead your men. And that is very fine. But that's the academic part of it. I think the fine points of being a good naval officer are something you almost pick up by osmosis if you are around the ridges long enough. It's a question of watching the way other people do business, seeing what works, seeing what doesn't work and learning from your mistakes.

A leader is a team member: "If we're sinking, can I trust the guy next to you?"

Bonding with your group is a powerful thread across all these ex-cadets' memories. The majority said they developed lifelong friendships with people in their groups. And the trust that developed from these links was an important part of leadership training. You had to learn to trust your team before you could lead them. Karen Peach, 1980s: "the girls had to both show that they could serve as leaders ... but also to be team members. ... People only think of leadership in the leadership role. But more is required than that."

People were bound by a common ethos. For Rodney Agar, 1940s:

If you join at the age of 13, you're imbued with what's called the spirit of the service ... and we thought of ourselves as The Service. ... The Navy was a hugely important part in the British way of life, it connected us with the whole of our Empire.

Leadership training was timeless; this photograph and others in this section were taken in the 1990s

… At Dartmouth, you were all part of that huge historical period in Britain's history.

Robert Griffiths, who came to the College in the 1950s at 17, put it differently: "You have a duty to lead, and your duty to lead overtakes absolutely everything else."

Teamwork was essential to survival in the pressured life of the College, as John Edge, 1980s, explains:

> We worked out early on that everybody had strengths and weaknesses. Some could polish shoes, some could write essays, some were really good at giving presentations. … When we went outdoors … and did leadership exercises, some people were really good at map reading, some were really good at tying knots and rigging shear legs … You mucked in together because that was the way to survive.

This pattern of behaviour learned as cadets held up under later pressure. Five decades earlier, Duncan Knight, 1930s, remembered that forcing "a group of … strangers … to live together, get on with each other, support each other and not let each other down … paid out during the war, [when] a group of officers were thrown together … had to work together, and had to take in each other's washing. Above all they had to obey the Captain."

The practical application: "They would dump a load of you on the moors"

There were major exercises on the river and Dartmoor when cadets practised leadership under difficult physical conditions. Henry Duffy, in the 1980s "did something called PLT's, Practical Leadership Tasks":

> You are given a command position and a task to move something from A to B with some constraints … an invisible chasm, or a chemical weapon, and you have to … galvanise a team, give a clear set of orders … in what is often very challenging circumstances. … It's a great 'opener' in terms of leadership development.

Terry Jane, 1960s, recalled being taught how to motivate others and learn self-confidence:

They would dump a load of you on the moors ... with a compass and a dodgy map, and it's rainy and cold and horrible, and [they'd give you a task]. ... And you'd get there cold and wet, and three of them are almost in tears because they don't like it and things are too heavy for you to carry and any normal person is going to say 'well I'm not going to do this, this is silly and I can't do it and they can't do it'. But you do, you're forced to and you force the ones that don't want to do it to do it. And that's where you start learning how to encourage other people. ... But later you realise actually what it's done for you. [When] you have much deeper challenges later in the services, you can look back and say 'well, this is ... not too much of a problem'.

"No doubt our character was greatly enhanced by doing that," says Australian Andrew Craig, 1960s; "And we all survived":

The exercise required [you] to carry your tent as a team of six or seven ... from point A to point B, Point B being one of the more prominent tors around Dartmoor. In, I might say the middle of winter, which was very cold, very wet and kind of miserable. The object of the exercise was that everybody had to pull his weight, carry the tent, rig the tent and make sure it stayed up. So that was probably a two to three day exercise. But somewhere in the middle of it, when the tent had blown down for the umpteenth time, we huddled around and said we are naval officers, why are we sitting in the middle of Dartmoor in a tent that keeps blowing down when we thought we were going to be at sea in a ship?

Women were fully integrated in naval training in 1993, but in 1980 they were already doing a leadership course on Dartmoor called Moor-Ex. "It was along the same lines as the men's, although conducted separately," remembers Karen Peach. "All the assessment and the teaching [was by] ... a mixture of ourselves and the male staff officers and senior ratings, so that the standard of training was guaranteed right across the board for everybody. So the leadership side, certainly, was very much on par with what the men did."

In a nice aside, Terry Jane, then a staff officer, remembered his predecessor telling him that "for some reason the girls didn't seem to be able to navigate terribly well across the moors. So if they were sent off by themselves you'd never see them again. So they always had a [male] staff officer ... who, when they purposefully walked in one direction, would just point in the other direction where they had to go. So that was a lot of fun."

"You can't take the risk out of this game"

"Was it dangerous?" asks Christopher Ayres of the 1970s exercises:

Not really. ... You were encouraged to explore the envelope in terms of what was possible within your own capability. And when I was there, nobody

Rock climbing

died. A few people got hurt. One group went out on Dartmoor when it was really snowing. And a couple of guys came back with the early onset of hypothermia and frostbite, that sort of thing. … I assume there must have been some form of assessment in the early days of what was safe and what wasn't safe for us.

Cadets generally had confidence that the staff knew the limits. Mike Sauvage, 1960s:

> There was an understanding that discipline was important in an organisation where things could be dangerous … So somebody who is more experienced than you has got to make the decisions at the end of the day. And … there are times when people have got to give orders, and that you've got to act immediately on them. If you don't, it might be too late, and I think … that was always accepted.

Henry Duffy says of the 1980s: "You can't take the risk out of this game. … Fighting and winning in operations is a risky business. But we … risk assess everything [now, whereas] I'm not convinced when I went through training there was such a mature approach to risk."

Be honest, face mistakes and learn from them: "I dropped four of my team in the River Dart"
Things can go wrong, as John Lippiett, 1960s, explains:

> You might be on Dartmoor or up around the playing fields, and you've got three planks, all of the wrong size, and a bit of rope and you've got to get from A to B carrying something over your shoulder. It's near impossible but not quite, and then you give it to [other] people to do. So one takes charge of half a dozen others … and it usually ends as a complete Horlicks.

And David Knight, ten years later, recalled: "I dropped four of my team in the River Dart trying to get them across. This was … probably towards the end of the first six weeks. … I didn't exactly ask them to tight-rope-walk across the water but I think my plan was a bit light. I think the raft I was in charge of sank as well."

Just as important as making mistakes was learning from them. Debriefing was key: "You can learn from it," said Lippiett, "you can debrief and see where you go wrong and then you can do something else and it goes right. So you can learn in a teaching environment, that's practical leadership."

Knight remembered:

> The … Divisional Officer shadowing you and taking notes would be reasonably straightforward and hard-hitting about it. 'That wasn't much good was it Mr Knight? What do you think went wrong there?' As long as you could come up with some sort of honest assessment you weren't going to get too badly dealt with. And eventually it sinks in and you become able to achieve these tasks.

The ability to make mistakes and learn from them was a key part of leadership training. "By all means make your mistakes and I think that is one of the great things in the service," said Andrew Craig, 1960s:

> As long as it is not an absolutely outrageously stupid mistake, people will give you credit for at least trying. You probably only want to do it once. But that's fine. And that doesn't necessarily happen in the civilian world these days. You screw up once in the civilian world and bad things can happen almost immediately. Mark you, if you screw up really badly in the Navy bad things can happen too. It's not a smart move to run your ship aground or crash your aircraft for no good reason. But if you have conducted yourself professionally and can argue the case of why you did what you did, then I think the Navy is prepared to listen to you.

Role models; "Leadership is the ability to inspire others"

Exemplary teachers made exemplary leaders. Paul Hart, 1980s, put it succinctly: "One thing that always sat on my mind was never ask anything of anybody which you can't do yourself. If you are not able to lead and demonstrate by example, then don't tell other people to do it."

"Learn from your betters," said Christopher Ayres, 1970s: "Learn from the ones around you, learn as a sailor, pick up all the skills as you go along. It takes time, and you learn and you come out at the end a better person."

Inspirational teachers of leadership were quoted by later cadets. Neil Blair and John Forbes had both been cadets at the College (and contributed to this project) and returned as Commanders.

Paul Rampling remembers learning self-confidence from Neil Blair during a sea exercise to the Channel Islands and back in the 1980s:

"I was in charge of the navigation, driving, piloting, everything. … It was a steep learning curve." Coming back to Dartmouth: "[It was] in the dark against a spring ebb, so a really strong current … and I had to put [this] big fishing vessel … in between two big expensive yachts." He remembered the Director of Studies suggesting to Blair that he take over: "And he said 'no, no, let him do it.' And I took it in. I'll never forget that … that is a real confidence builder. … Somebody had faith in my ability. … That's how they inspire you to do well in the future."

"In a terrible situation … humour has always helped me"

John Forbes , a cadet in the 1930s, had said: "I'm a great believer in teaching by example and when you are spending almost four years in what was a naval atmosphere with handpicked officers you are bound to get what I call a brush off from them."

And he must have applied his beliefs because 30 years later it was just this "brush off" from Forbes that John Madgwick recalled in the 1960s.

Forbes, then a Commander, had a mini-Moke, an early type of beach-buggy, and after a post-Dartmoor mess dinner, Madgwick and his group decided it would be a good idea to "move the mini-Moke from the ramps to the deck outside the Commander's office, which was two decks up via the quarterdeck." So they did. At 3 am, they were woken and told "'the Commander wants his car back on the ramps and he wants it now.' … It was a lot more difficult to get it down than it was to get it up. But we got it back onto the ramps. At which point the Commander got in the car, did a celebratory circuit of the ramps and went off to his house. And so honour was satisfied on both sides." What Madgwick took away from the incident was that humorous tolerance was an important part of leadership:

> He could see that these merry japes were bound to happen but by handling it in just the right way … everybody realised they had gone far enough. … When I had my own ships later on, as a result of that particular episode, one allowed the team to have a little bit of leeway before one clamped down on them. … One has to be able to relax a little bit and blow off steam occasionally.

Measuring success: Oily Qs

Joe Young, 1950s, recalls being marked on "officer-like qualities":

… which we all used to call 'Oily Q*s*', a good name really. We had one chap who was so 'officer-like quality' dominated, we used to call him Oily Dom, his first name being Dom. But it all became a bit of a joke, and if you really wanted to insult somebody, you could always [call him] … Oily Q*s*. And how they put the marks together, I don't know. Just by watching, I suppose, and saying, 'Well, he's never going to make it' or, 'He'll never get the hang of this, that or the other.'

Andrew Craig, ten years later, imagined something similar:

> Oh yes. officer-like qualities. And we were marked on them as well. That was probably the greatest mystery of the whole of our life because we were never, never really told how the hell they were judged. … I suspect at the end of the term all those who assessed us sat around a big table and said, 'Andrew Craig, well how do you think he performed?' 'Ooh, he has done alright but on such and such a day he didn't do too well because of this, that and the other thing and he really screwed this up because he bawled out a young cadet when he shouldn't have and therefore we mark him at this mark. But on the other hand he seems to have learned so maybe we give him a few more marks for the dreaded officer-like qualities.' … You could certainly fail the course for want of the undefined baseline of officer-like qualities.

"Three planks, all of the wrong size"

What did cadets believe they learnt?: "The Navy got me doing things that I never thought I could possibly do"

Jock Slater, in the 1950s, learnt the importance of really knowing his team:

> The key to a successful career, and I learned this at Dartmouth, is to surround yourself with people of great quality and delegate to them mercilessly … And that's the key. … What you learned at Dartmouth was [about] … people – their strengths, their weaknesses, their successes, their failures. I was lucky enough to be the senior midshipman … and learned a tremendous amount [about] the broader elements of leadership. And that stayed with me for the rest of my career. I was lucky enough [to have] three or four commands, including an aircraft carrier. And a lot of the early standards and style I learned in the seven terms I did at Dartmouth.

John Lippiett, 1960s, absorbed communication skills that he applied in the Falklands: "I saw my role as getting around the ship, boosting people, reassuring them, communicating and so on. Leadership in war, while the fighting goes on and everyone's doing their job, is to maintain morale. … It goes back to initial training."

Like Paul Rampling in his sea exercise, Christopher Ayres, 1970s, remembered learning self-confidence and how to make decisions when tired and stressed:

> The subliminal message was, you are doing these activities … to give yourself confidence that they can be done and that you personally can do them. And … you get used to making decisions when you are tired and under stress. In consequence, your decision-making process gets better. … I think … it had always been done that way.

And Robert Griffiths, 1950s, says:

> One of the extraordinary things about the Navy was it got me doing things that I never thought I could possibly do. It even got me to go over the top of a box horse without landing on my face. That was teaching us that because you're in the Navy you can do anything. And that's a very useful lesson. You never think, 'Gosh, this is going to be too difficult for me.' You think, 'Well, I was in the Navy, I could have a go at that.'

Samson Mwathethe, 1970s, learnt how to be just:

> One thing I remember is that when somebody makes a mistake, you should be able as a leader to determine whether it was intended or [not]. … Because you are the boss, you can punish. … But if you are able to tell that a mistake was an error, you should be able to leave that alone.

THE REAL TEST OF TRAINING

Jogged by recollections and prompted by questions, the records of the former cadets interviewed for this project have common threads, despite all the complexities of individual experiences. When you look back over these themes, a coherence emerges, not only in the ethos behind the training, the sense of duty and service, but also in its practical purpose.

Training at the College was a preparation for war, or "life at sea on a warship", as the Duke of Edinburgh put it. Cadets there in the 1930s and early 1940s were well aware of this. But after 1945 few former cadets seem to have expected another global conflict. Yet many were to serve in smaller, although no less deadly, disputes, including the Falklands in 1982. If you compare their recollections of Dartmouth with their memories of the qualities called for in the Falklands, you can see how the training described in this booklet through so many voices met this ultimate test.

David Hart-Dyke, at the College in the 1960s, was Captain of HMS *Coventry* and Neil Hall, 1980s, was a junior officer in a frigate that joined the war just as *Coventry* was sunk.

Both Hart-Dyke and Hall said that trust, discipline and the humour and comradeship that fed into morale were core. The mind-set these produced allowed people to act in extremely dangerous conditions with unquestioning promptness, reliability and endurance. Both attributed this achievement to their training. Hall remembers that when the action started, "the training … just took over."

Throughout their time at the College, cadets were absorbing the importance of learning to trust each other. Almost always, they were in teams. In that hectic first term, on Dartmoor or river exercises many recorded they could only survive by helping each other. This learned experience led directly to the automatic teamwork of captain, officer and crew in a ship under fire. Cadets had learned to be team members as well as leaders.

The discipline that meant immediate and automatic responses to orders despite the surrounding mayhem, when "all of a sudden you're just concentrating on what you are meant to be doing", were developed at Dartmouth. That endless drilling on the parade ground or during those early

Passing-out Parades have changed little. This is the Parade in 2016

morning exercises, the apparently stupid micro-management, the rules on folding clothes, what to wear when, and, particularly, the relentless focus on punctuality.

The self-discipline that kept you going on ridiculously challenging training exercises taught you to persist in the face of danger. Hall describes exactly how not wanting to appear a wimp when you're cold, tired, and hungry with miles still to go on Dartmoor transcribed to enduring his first air raid: "Was it frightening? No. It was terrifying. But I looked around. Everyone was looking around. And everyone was thinking, well he's not looking frightened, he's not frightened. But everyone is. But you just, you don't want to seem to be frightened in front of your friends."

The camaraderie and the humour that belonged to it resurface again and again in the memories of former cadets. Practical jokes, the tolerance of them and parade-ground joking at Dartmouth were reborn at war as trench humour and comradeship that fed into the morale that enabled extraordinary courage. Hart-Dyke's ship, *HMS Coventry*, sank in 20 minutes and "it was the young people in the ship's company who actually took charge. Hardly a word was spoken but they ... went down again and again to rescue people."

At the end, said Hart-Dyke, "when I came back, I was amazed with the fuss that was made about all this. ... We were just doing the job that we were trained to do. We didn't think it was a big deal."

The training that former cadets describe in this booklet has shown how the College was able to adapt to times of great change. But it also records how the College's fundamental purpose, to produce officers prepared to die for their country, has remained the same.

APPENDIX AND PERSON INDEX

Former naval officer cadets interviewed for Oral History Project, 2012–17
(By decade of attendance at the Royal Naval College; page numbers next to names identify quotations in the text)

1930s

Lieutenant Commander Rupert Craven 24, 38

HRH The Duke of Edinburgh 11, 67

Lieutenant Commander Anthony Fletcher 26

Vice Admiral Sir John Forbes 14, 16, 17, 18, 33, 36, 37, 63, 64

Lieutenant Adrian Holloway 14, 15, 16, 17, 28, 45, 46

Vice Admiral Sir James Jungius 14, 15, 19, 23, 27, 36, 37, 50

Captain Duncan Knight 19, 45, 46, 52, 60

Captain Anthony McCrum 13, 14, 15, 35, 39, 41, 46, 50, 51, 54, 55

Admiral Sir William O'Brien 15, 26, 37, 41, 42, 51, 55

Admiral Sir John Treacher 18, 30

Commander Derek Willan 26, 59

1940s

Commander Rodney Agar 20, 51, 59

Lieutenant Commander John G. Davies 18

Captain Michael Fulford-Dobson 39, 42

Vice Admiral Sir Robert Gerken

Lieutenant Tom Gullick

Captain Patrick Harland 20, 21, 22, 34, 48

Captain Richard Hill 25, 47, 51

Captain Murray Johnstone 22

Commander Julian Loring 40, 48

Commander William Melly 20, 21, 22, 36, 37, 38, 40, 51

Captain Rolfe Monteith 14, 15, 16, 47

Lieutenant Commander Ian Pearson

Lieutenant Commander Tom Potts 24, 40, 52

Commander Colin Traill 27

Lieutenant Commander Jolyon Waterfield 22, 48, 54

1950s

Captain Neil Blair 28, 42, 45, 63, 64,

Lieutenant Commander Robert Griffiths 60, 66

Captain Jock Morrison 23, 34, 39, 53, 56

Captain David Lucas Phillips 35, 53

Commander David Price 35, 43, 46, 56

Admiral Sir Jock Slater 37, 39, 66

Vice Admiral Sir Jonathan Tod 24, 36, 52, 56

Captain David Wixon 42

Commander Joe Young 28, 36, 45, 47, 64

1960s

Commander Peter Booth 33, 38, 47, 52

Rear Admiral Roy Clare

Captain Andrew Craig 25, 36, 43, 50, 57, 59, 61, 63, 65

Captain David Hart-Dyke 67, 69

Commander Terry Jane 24, 57, 60, 61

Commander David Lingard 37, 58

Rear Admiral John Lippiett 28, 56, 62, 63, 66

Commodore John Madgwick 25, 53, 64

Nigel Reilly

Captain Paul Robinson

Captain Mike Sauvage 62

1970s

Commander Christopher Ayres 25, 33, 36, 47, 53, 58, 61, 63, 66

Commander David Carpenter 23, 24, 29, 56

Commodore Michael Cochrane 28, 31, 45, 50, 55

Stephen Daltrey 48

Second Officer Judy Faulkner 45, 49

Commander David Knight 34, 56, 63

Robin Morello

General Samson Mwathethe 34, 66

HRH The Prince Andrew 8, 11, 33, 43, 49, 59

Commodore Carolyn Stait 29, 53

Lieutenant Commander Cliff Williams 26

1980s

Commander Mark (Dicky) Barton 25, 27, 43, 57,

Captain Iain Cull 34, 58

Captain Henry Duffy 26, 60, 62

Commander John Edge 31, 34, 37, 60

Commander Neil (Nobby) Hall 67, 69

Lieutenant Commander Paul Hart 31, 55, 63

First Officer Karen Peach 41, 59, 61

Lieutenant Paul Rampling 27, 38, 63, 66

Lieutenant Commander Nichola Winstanley 26, 29, 30, 54

ACKNOWLEDGEMENTS

The OHP Committee of the Britannia Museum Trust, and especially Fiona Clampin, David Craddock, Helen Darch, Commander Robert Dunn, Dr Jane Harrold, Sir Geoffrey Newman, Commodore Chris Peach, Dr Richard Porter, Admiral Robin Shiffner, Julia Springett and Carolyn Steen; and Pierre Landell-Mills

Dr Richard Porter, Dr Jane Harrold and Craig Keating were instrumental in providing the illustrations, as was Nicko Franks in finding the photograph of Mark Sugden

RELATED INFORMATION

Extracts from the audio recordings of the Britannia's Voices interviews and their full transcripts will be available on the Britannia Association website: http://www.britanniaassociation.org.uk

Harrold J & Porter R, *Britannia Royal Naval College Dartmouth: An Illustrated History* (Richard Webb, 3rd edn, 2012)

Harrold J, "Britannia's Voices: An Oral History of Officer Training at the Britannia Royal Naval College", *Revue Maritime,* Paris, publication due